CAVENDISH lawcards series

Criminal Law

Third Edition

Cavendish
Publishing
Limited

London • Sydney

Third edition first published 2002 by Cavendish Publishing Limited, The Glass House, Wharton Street, London WC1X 9PX, United Kingdom

Telephone: +44 (0)20 7278 8000
Facsimile: +44 (0)20 7278 8080
Email: info@cavendishpublishing.com
Website: www.cavendishpublishing.com

© Cavendish Publishing Limited 2002

First edition 1996
Second edition 1999
Reprinted 2000
Third edition 2002

All rights reserved. No part of this publication may be reproduced, stored in a retrieval system, or transmitted in any form or by any means, electronic, mechanical, photocopying, recording, scanning or otherwise, except under the terms of the Copyright Designs and Patents Act 1988 or under the terms of a licence issued by the Copyright Licensing Agency, 90 Tottenham Court Road, London W1P 9HE, UK, without the prior permission in writing of the publisher.

British Library Cataloguing in Publication Data

Criminal law – 3rd ed – (Law cards)
1 Criminal law – England 2 Criminal law – Wales
345.4'2

ISBN 1 85941 515 6
Printed and bound in Great Britain

Contents

1 The nature of a crime — 1

2 Inchoate offences and participation — 19

3 Non-fatal offences against the person — 43

4 Fatal offences — 55

5 Offences against property — 69

6 General defences — 99

1 The nature of a crime

A crime is conduct which has been defined as such by statute or by common law.

Generally, a person may not be convicted of a crime unless he has acted in a proscribed way (that is, the *actus reus*) with a defined state of mind (that is, the *mens rea*). The main exception to this are crimes of strict liability where no *mens rea* need be proved.

CRIME = *ACTUS REUS* + *MENS REA*
+ ABSENCE OF A VALID DEFENCE

The prosecution must prove the existence of the *actus reus* and *mens rea* beyond reasonable doubt. This is sometimes referred to as the *Woolmington* rule (*Woolmington v DPP* (1935)).

The classification of criminal law

- Criminal law
  - General Principles
    - *Actus reus*
      - Causation
      - Omissions
      - Willed conduct
      - State of affairs
    - *Mens rea*
      - Intention
      - Recklessness
      - Negligence
      - Blamelessness
  - Inchoate offences
    - Incitement
    - Conspiracy
    - Attempt
  - Offences against the person
    - Non-fatal
      - Assault and battery
      - OAPA 1861, s 47
      - OAPA 1861, s 20
      - OAPA 1861, s 18
      - Sexual offences
    - Fatal
      - Murder
      - Manslaughter
  - Offences against property
    - Theft
    - Robbery
    - Burglary
    - Criminal damage
    - Deception
    - Handling
  - Participation

```
                    ┌──► Provocation
          ┌──────┐  │
     ┌───►│Voluntary├──► Diminished responsibility
     │    └──────┘  │
     │              ├──► Suicide pact
     │              │
     │              └──► Infanticide
     │
     │              ┌──► Constructive manslaughter
     │  ┌────────┐  │
     ├─►│Involuntary├─► Killing by gross negligence
     │  └────────┘  │
     │              ├──► Motor manslaughter
     │              │
     │              └──► Causing death by dangerous driving
     │
     │              ┌──► s 15(1) of the TA 1968 (property)
     │              │
     │              ├──► s 16 of the TA 1968 (pecuniary adv)
     │              │
     ├──────────────┼──► s 1(1) of the TA 1978 (services)
     │              │
     │              ├──► s 2 of the TA 1978 (evasion of liability)
     │              │
     │              └──► s 15A of the TA 1968 (money transfer)
     │
     │              ┌──► The principal
     │              │
     │              ├──► The accomplice
     │              │
     │              ├──► Joint principals
     │              │
     └──────────────┼──► Joint enterprise
                    │
                    ├──► Innocent agency
                    │
                    ├──► *Actus reus*
                    │
                    └──► *Mens rea*
```

CRIMINAL LAW

3

Characteristics of an *actus reus*

Definition
An *actus reus* consists of all the elements in the statutory or common law definition of the offence except the defendant's mental element.

Analysis of the actus reus
An *actus reus* can be identified by looking at the definition of the offence in question and subtracting the *mens rea* requirements of 'knowingly', 'intentionally', 'recklessly', 'maliciously', 'dishonestly' or 'negligently'.

ACTUS REUS = DEFINITION OF THE OFFENCE – *MENS REA*

Once the *actus reus* has been identified, it can be further analysed into the central conduct of the offence, the surrounding circumstances in which it must take place and any requisite consequences.

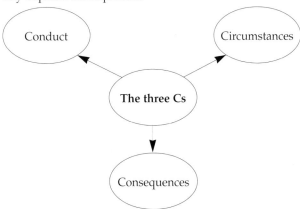

This process of identifying and analysing an *actus reus* can be illustrated in relation to s 1(1) of the Criminal Damage Act 1971 which provides:

> A person who without lawful excuse destroys or damages any property belonging to another intending to destroy or damage any such property or being reckless as to whether such property would be destroyed or damaged shall be guilty of an offence.

Once expressions relating to the *mens rea* requirements of intention or recklessness have been subtracted, the *actus reus* consists of destroying or damaging property belonging to another.

CONDUCT	= the act of destroying or damaging
CIRCUMSTANCES	= the fact that the property must belong to another
CONSEQUENCES	= the resultant damage or destruction

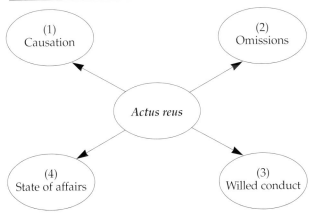

(1) Causation

If the definition of an offence specifies a particular consequence, then it is a 'result' crime and the prosecution must prove, in order to establish the *actus reus*, that the defendant *caused* that consequence.

For example, in order to establish the *actus reus* of an offence of homicide, it is necessary to prove that the defendant caused the death of the victim.

Causation in fact
The first step in establishing causation is to ask 'was the defendant's act a *cause in fact* of the specified consequence (for example, death in the case of homicide)?'. This question can be answered by asking: 'But for what the defendant did would the consequence have occurred?' If the answer is no, the result would not have occurred but for what the defendant did and, therefore, causation in fact is established.

An example where the prosecution failed to establish causation in fact is the case of *R v White* (1910). The defendant had put cyanide into his mother's drink, but the medical evidence showed that she died of heart failure before the poison could take effect. Consequently, the answer to the question 'But for what the defendant did would she have died?' is 'yes'. She would have died anyway.

Causation in law
Just because the prosecution establish that the defendant's act was a cause in fact of the prohibited consequence, does not necessarily mean that the defendant is liable. It is also necessary to prove that the defendant's act was a cause in law of the specified consequence.

One approach to establishing causation in law is to consider whether the defendant's act was an 'operative and substantial' cause of the consequence in question. Only if the defendant's act could be said to have merely provided the setting in which some other cause operated would the chain of causation be broken (*R v Smith* (1959)).

It should be noted that 'substantial', in this context, simply means more than a very trivial cause which would be ignored under the *de minimis* principle.

Moreover, an 'operative' cause need not be the sole or main cause of the specified consequence (*R v Benge* (1865)).

An alternative approach to the 'operative and substantial' test for establishing causation in law is to consider whether the result specified in the *actus reus* was a reasonably foreseeable consequence of what the defendant had done. Thus, in *R v Pagett* (1983), the defendant was held to have caused the death of a girl hostage he was holding in front of him when he fired at armed police officers who returned fire, killing the girl. It was reasonably foreseeable in the circumstances that the officers would instinctively return fire and hit the victim.

The 'thin skull' rule

Even if injury or death is not a reasonably foreseeable consequence of the defendant's act, he would still in law have caused that result if the victim suffered from some physical or mental condition that made him or her especially vulnerable. This is known as the 'thin skull' rule which provides that the defendant must take his victim as he finds him. For example, in *R v Blaue* (1975), the defendant was held to have caused the death of a Jehovah's Witness who he had stabbed, notwithstanding that she had refused a blood transfusion that would have probably saved her life. He had to take his victim as he found her, including not just her physical condition, but also her religious beliefs.

Self-neglect

Similarly, although it may not be reasonably foreseeable that the victim will neglect his wounds, it seems that such neglect will not break the chain of causation (*R v Smith* (1959)). Even if the victim aggravates the condition caused by the defendant, the chain of causation will not be broken (*R v Dear* (1996)).

Death caused by medical treatment

Where death is caused by the medical treatment of a wound, the original attacker is held liable for homicide. This is so even in the case of *negligent* medical treatment (*R v Smith* (1959)).

However, it seems that 'palpably wrong' medical treatment will break the chain of causation (*R v Jordan* (1956)). In *R v Cheshire* (1991), it was stated that, unless the negligent treatment was 'so independent of the accused's acts' and 'so potent in causing death' that the contribution made by his acts was insignificant, the chain of causation would not be broken (and see *Mellor* (1996)).

There is some authority for the suggestion that the administration of pain saving drugs which incidentally shorten life by a very short period (hours or days, but not weeks or months) would not amount to a cause in law of death (*R v Adams* (1957)).

```
                          START
                            │
                            ▼
         ┌──────────────────────────────────┐
         │ But for what the defendant did,  │  Yes
         │ would the result still have      ├──────▶ No causation
         │ occurred? (R v White (1910))     │
         └──────────────────────────────────┘
                            │ No
                            ▼
         ┌──────────────────────────────────┐
         │ Was the result reasonably        │  Yes
         │ foreseeable? (R v Pagett (1983)) ├──────▶ Causation established
         └──────────────────────────────────┘
                            │ No
                            ▼
         ┌──────────────────────────────────┐
         │ Did the victim suffer from a     │  Yes
         │ 'thin skull'? (R v Blaue (1975)) ├──────▶ Causation established
         └──────────────────────────────────┘
                            │ No
                            ▼                                Was the
         ┌──────────────────────────────────┐  Yes        treatment        Yes
         │ Were the injuries exacerbated    ├──────▶   'palpably wrong'?  ──────▶ No causation
         │ by medical treatment?            │           (R v Jordan (1956))
         └──────────────────────────────────┘                  │ No
                            │ No                               ▼
                            ▼                          Causation established
                                                          (R v Smith (1959))
         ┌──────────────────────────────────┐
         │ Were the injuries exacerbated    │  Yes
         │ by self-neglect? (R v Dear (1996))├─────▶ Causation established
         └──────────────────────────────────┘
                            │ No
                            ▼
                      No causation
```

(2) Omissions

As a general rule, a person is not criminally liable for what they do not do. However, there are exceptions where the defendant is under a positive duty to act. In these exceptional situations, the defendant will have caused the *actus reus* by doing nothing.

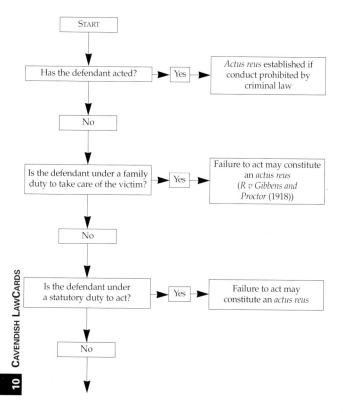

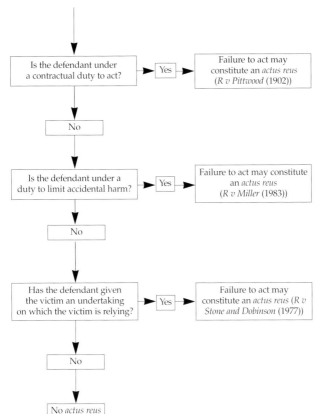

(3) The conduct must be willed

Where, as is usually the case, the *actus reus* of an offence specifies some form of conduct, it must be proved that the defendant consciously willed the relevant action.

If the defendant's muscles acted without the control of his mind he is not blameworthy and will be able to plead automatism (*Bratty v AG for Northern Ireland* (1963)).

Evidence of an 'external factor' is crucial to establish a plea of automatism (*R v Quick* (1973); *R v Sullivan* (1984)). Where the cause of the behaviour is 'internal', such as a 'disease of the mind' or a disease of the body, the relevant defence will be that of insanity rather than automatism (*R v Hennessy* (1989)).

Impaired, reduced or partial control by the defendant will not found a defence of automatism. A total loss of voluntary control is required (*AG's Reference (No 2 of 1992)* (1993)).

If the defendant is at fault in bringing about the autonomic state, for example, by voluntarily taking dangerous drugs, he will have a defence to crimes of 'specific intent', but not to those of 'basic intent' (*R v Lipman* (1970); *R v Bailey* (1983)).

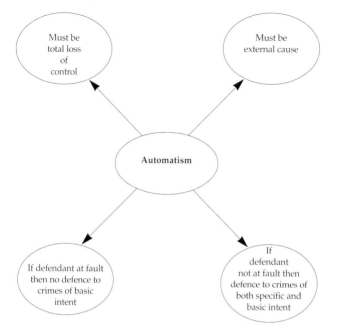

(4) State of affairs offences

A crime may be so defined so as not to require any willed action at all; it may be enough if a specified 'state of affairs' is proved to exist. For example, s 4 of the Road Traffic Act 1988 provides that a person who, when in charge of a motor vehicle on a road or other public place, is unfit to drive through drink or drugs, commits an offence. It is not the action of taking charge of the vehicle or that of *becoming* unfit which constitutes the offence, but simply the state of *being unfit*.

Thus, the defendant in *R v Larsonneur* (1933) was convicted of being found in the UK, contrary to the Aliens Order of 1920, despite the fact that she had been forcibly brought into the jurisdiction by the immigration authorities.

Similarly, the defendant in *Winzar v Chief Constable of Kent* (1983) was convicted of being found drunk on the highway, despite the fact that he had been deposited there by police officers.

'State of affairs' offences are often also offences of 'strict liability' (see below). It is not surprising that they tend to be regarded as unjustifiably harsh, since not only is there no need to prove any action by the defendant, but also there is no need to prove any *mens rea* either.

The nature of *mens rea*

Definition

The term *mens rea* refers to the mental element in the definition of a crime. This mental element is usually denoted by words such as 'intentionally', 'knowingly', 'recklessly', 'maliciously' or 'negligently'.

The main forms of *mens rea* are as follows:

- **Mens rea**
  - **Intention**
    - Direct (the defendant desires a consequence and it is his purpose to achieve it).
    - A result is indirectly intended even though it is not desired, when:
      (1) that result is a virtually certain consequence; and
      (2) the actor knows that it is a virtually certain consequence (*R v Hancock and Shankland* (1986); *R v Nedrick* (1986); *R v Woollin* (1998)).
  - **Recklessness**
    - *Cunningham* (the conscious taking of an unjustified risk (*R v Cunningham* (1957))).
    - *Caldwell* (the conscious or unconscious taking of an obvious risk (*MPC v Caldwell* (1982))).
  - Gross negligence – defendant owes a duty of care – breaches that duty – creates a risk of death – breach of duty is so gross it deserves to be described as 'criminal' (*R v Adomako* (1995)).

Blamelessness

A person is blameless if they have acted reasonably in the circumstances. However, even 'blameless' behaviour can attract criminal sanctions in the case of crimes of strict liability.

Transferred malice

If the defendant, with the *mens rea* of a particular crime, does an act which causes the *actus reus* of the same crime, he is guilty, even though the result, in some respects, is an unintended one (*R v Latimer* (1886)).

However, if the defendant, with the *mens rea* of a particular crime, does an act which causes the *actus reus* of another crime, he will not be liable under the doctrine of transferred malice (*R v Pembliton* (1874)).

Transferred malice 1

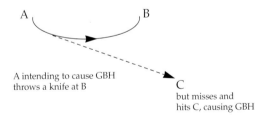

A intending to cause GBH throws a knife at B

but misses and hits C, causing GBH

A is guilty of causing GBH to C under the doctrine of transferred malice since he has caused the *actus reus* of an offence with the requisite *mens rea* for the same offence.

Transferred malice 2

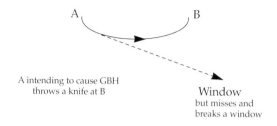

A is not guilty of criminal damage to the window; the doctrine of transferred malice does not operate since he has caused the *actus reus* of one offence with the *mens rea* of a different offence (however, if the prosecution proved that A was reckless in relation to damaging the window by throwing an object in the vicinity, then he would be liable under normal principles).

In *AG's Reference (No 3 of 1994)* (1997), the House of Lords confirmed the existence of the doctrine of transferred malice, but declined to extend the principle to what it regarded as a 'double transfer' of intent. In this case, the defendant had stabbed a woman whom he knew to be pregnant. She recovered, but there was evidence that the child was born prematurely as a result of the wound to the mother and, as a result of the premature birth, died 120 days later. The House of Lords considered this case to involve a 'double transfer' of intent from the mother to the foetus and from the foetus to the child.

Coincidence of *actus reus* and *mens rea*

The *mens rea* must coincide at some point in time with the act which causes the *actus reus* (*R v Jakeman* (1983)). However, the courts are sometimes prepared to hold that the *actus reus* consisted of a continuing act and that the defendant is liable if he formed the requisite *mens rea* at some point during this continuing act (*R v Thabo Meli* (1954); *R v Church* (1966)).

It seems that the continuing act will continue for as long as the defendant is about the business of committing or covering up the crime (*R v Le Brun* (1992) and see *AG's Reference (No 3 of 1994)* (1997)).

D	*Actus reus*	*Mens rea*
Does act without *mens rea*	✔	✘
Act continues		
Forms *mens rea* at a later stage		✔

Defendant liable under the continuing act doctrine.

Ignorance or mistake of law

Ignorance of the *criminal law* is no defence, but a mistake of *civil law* may be a defence to a criminal charge, provided it negates the *mens rea* for the offence in question (*R v Esop* (1836); *R v Smith* (1974)).

2 Inchoate offences and participation

Inchoate liability can occur where the defendant progresses some way towards the commission of an offence, but does not necessarily commit the completed offence.

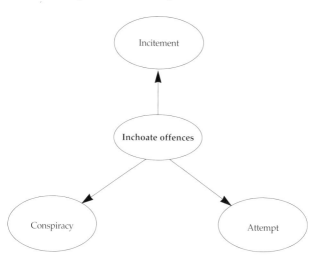

The prosecution have the discretion to charge a defendant with an inchoate offence, even where the completed offence appears to have been committed. This strategy might be adopted where there are likely to be evidential problems with pursuing a prosecution for the full offence.

On the other hand, the prosecution are not at liberty to charge a defendant with *both* an inchoate offence and a completed crime in relation to the same criminal act.

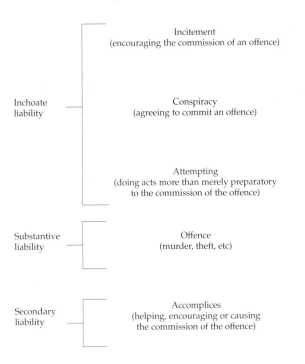

However, where the completed offence is committed, a person who has incited or conspired to commit that offence will become a participant and could incur liability as an accomplice.

Incitement at common law

Definition
An incitement consists of encouraging or pressurising another to commit an offence. The defendant is the incitor. The person he seeks to incite is the incitee.

Actus reus
The central conduct of the offence can take various forms, such as suggesting, proposing, requesting, encouraging, persuading, threatening or pressurising another to commit an offence (*Race Relations Board v Applin* (1973)).

It is necessary that the incitement is communicated to the incitee (*R v Banks* (1873)), but there is no need for the incitee to act on the incitement (*R v Higgins* (1801)).

If the incitor tries, but fails, to communicate the incitement, then he would be liable of the offence of attempted incitement (*R v Ransford* (1874)).

There is no need to prove that the incitee has the same *mens rea* as the incitor (*DPP v Armstrong* (2000)), but the incitee must be proved to have been aware of the circumstances that constitute the offence – that is, if the incitor suggests to the incitee that she should collect welfare benefit payments to which she is not entitled, it must be shown that the incitee was aware of the fact that she was not so entitled (*R v Curr* (1968)).

A member of a class of people that a particular offence is designed to protect cannot be liable for inciting that offence (*R v Tyrrell* (1894)). Thus, a girl under the age of 16 could not be guilty of inciting a man to have sexual intercourse with her since she is a victim that the offence of unlawful sexual intercourse is designed to protect.

Mens rea

The defendant must intend to incite and intend that the incitee act on the incitement (*Invicta Plastics v Clare* (1976)).

In addition, the defendant must know of all the circumstances of the act incited which are elements of the crime in question and intend the consequences specified in the *actus reus*.

Since the *mens rea* of the person incited is included among the elements of the crime, the incitor must know or believe that the incitee has the requisite *mens rea* for the offence in question (*R v Curr* (1968)).

It follows that, if the defendant believes that the incitee will do the suggested act without the *mens rea* for the crime in question, then he is not guilty of incitement (even if, unknown to him, the incitee does have the necessary *mens rea*). In these circumstances, the defendant may be liable for the completed crime, either as an abettor or as a principal offender via the doctrine of innocent agency.

Impossibility

Incitement is a common law offence so the common law rules on impossibility apply – incitement is not governed by the Criminal Attempts Act 1981. The incitor is dealt with on the facts as he believes them to be. If the incitor suggests that an incitee should handle stolen goods but, unknown to the incitor, at the time of the incitement the goods have been restored to their lawful owner and thus can no longer, in law, be stolen goods, the incitor could still be guilty of inciting the offence of handling stolen goods – he believes the offence can be committed (*R v McDonough* (1962)).

Where what is incited is 'totally impossible' in the sense that it is something that no person could ever achieve (for example, the incitor suggests to the incitee that he should kill Queen Victoria), impossibility might still be available as a defence. The courts distinguish between an incitement that cannot be carried out because of a supervening event making its completion impossible, and one that could not in any circumstances result in an offence being committed (*R v Fitzmaurice* (1983), applying principles developed in relation to common law conspiracy by the House of Lords in *DPP v Nock* (1978)).

Incitement and other inchoate offences

As we have noted, there is an offence of attempted incitement (*R v Ransford* (1874)), but it seems that there is no offence of inciting an attempt (Sched 1, paras 34 and 35 of the Magistrates' Courts Act 1980).

The old common law offence of incitement to conspire was abolished by s 5(7) of the Criminal Law Act 1977, but there may be a conspiracy to incite.

At common law, the offence of inciting incitement exists (*R v Sirat* (1986)). However, as we have seen, s 5(7) of the Criminal Law Act 1977 abolished the offence of inciting conspiracy. It follows that the common law offence of inciting an incitement will now only exist where the incitement is based on threats or pressure which do not amount to an incitement to conspire (*R v Evans* (1986)).

Incitement and participation
Section 30(4) of the Criminal Law Act 1977 appears to have been drafted on the assumption that there is no such offence as incitement to counsel or abet an offence.

Conspiracy

Section 1(1) of the Criminal Law Act 1977 created a statutory offence of conspiracy and abolished, with two exceptions, the old common law offence of conspiracy.

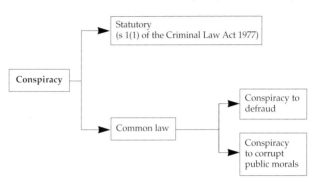

Statutory conspiracy

Definition
The statutory offence of conspiracy is created by s 1(1) of the Criminal Law Act 1977, as amended by s 5 of the Criminal Attempts Act 1981, which provides:

... if a person agrees with any other person or persons that a course of conduct shall be pursued which, if the agreement is carried out in accordance with their intentions, either:

(a) will necessarily amount to or involve the commission of any offence or offences by one or more of the parties to the agreement; or

(b) would do so but for the existence of facts which render the commission of the offence or any of the offences impossible, he is guilty of conspiracy to commit the offence or offences in question.

Actus reus

The *actus reus* of a statutory conspiracy consists of an agreement on a 'course of conduct' that will necessarily involve the commission of an offence.

It appears that merely talking about the possibility of committing an offence is not sufficient to constitute an agreement (*R v O'Brien* (1974)).

Section 1(1), para (b) of the Criminal Law Act 1977 makes it clear that, as far as *statutory* conspiracy is concerned, the fact that the agreement is impossible to carry out is no bar to liability (impossibility may still be a defence to a charge of common law conspiracy).

The agreement must be communicated between the parties to the conspiracy (*R v Scott* (1979)). However, it is not necessary for every party to a conspiracy to be aware of the existence of every other party. The agreement can take the form of a *chain*, where A agrees with B who then agrees with C and so on, a *wheel*, where numerous parties agree on the same course of conduct with one central figure or a *cluster*, where several parties simultaneously agree.

Chain

A   B   C

    AGREES WITH   WHO AGREES WITH

Wheel

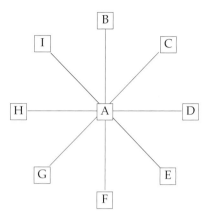

Cluster

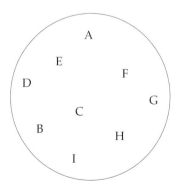

A person cannot be guilty of conspiracy to commit an offence if he is an intended victim of that offence (s 2(1) of the Criminal Law Act 1977).

A person shall not be guilty of conspiracy if the only other person with whom he agrees is his spouse (s 2(2)(a)); a child under the age of 10 (s 2(2)(b)); or an intended victim of the agreed offence (s 2(2)(c)).

If the words 'necessarily amount to ... the commission of any offence' were construed strictly, it would be impossible to secure any convictions for conspiracies to commit *possible* offences. For example, suppose that A agrees with B to put a deadly poison into C's food. At first sight, this appears to be a clear case of conspiracy to murder, but it could be argued that this course of conduct would not *necessarily* have amounted to the offence in question; C might not be hungry, or might drop the plate or might not die. Paradoxically, if the offence was impossible, perhaps because C was already dead at the time of the agreement, then there would be liability for conspiracy to murder since, as we have seen, impossibility is no defence.

In order to avoid this kind of anomalous result, the courts have been prepared to interpret the phrase 'course of conduct' in a way which includes not just the conspirators' intended actions, but also the intended consequences of those actions (*R v Reed* (1982)). According to this interpretation, A and B would be guilty of conspiracy to murder since the intended result of their common plan was the death of C.

Mens rea
The defendant must intend to agree on the commission of a particular offence and intend that the offence should be committed.

In addition, the defendant must know or believe the circumstances specified in the definition of the offence to exist and must intend that the prohibited consequences occur.

Intention is required even where the offence agreed upon is capable of being committed with a lesser degree of *mens rea* (*R v Siracusa* (1989)). For example, murder can be committed with an intention to kill or cause grievous bodily harm, but to be guilty of a conspiracy to murder nothing less than an intention to kill is required.

It is sometimes suggested that Lord Bridge, in *R v Anderson* (1986), held that it is not necessary to prove that the defendant intended the offence to be committed, merely that there was an intention to play some part in the carrying out of the agreement. However, the courts have tended to reinterpret, or clarify, Lord Bridge's comments in a way which makes it clear that there is no need for the prosecution to prove an intention to play a part in the common plan (*R v Siracusa* (1989); *R v Edwards* (1991)). It would now appear that a conspirator can play a part simply by agreeing that others should carry out the offence.

Common law conspiracy

Section 5(2) and (3) of the Criminal Law Act 1977 preserves two forms of common law conspiracy: conspiracy to defraud and conspiracy to corrupt public morals or outrage public decency.

Conspiracy to defraud

Many fraudulent activities will constitute substantive criminal offences and an agreement to engage in them could be charged as a statutory conspiracy. However, some fraudulent activities may not amount to a substantive offence. An agreement to engage in this kind of activity cannot be charged as a statutory conspiracy, but may well result in a conviction for common law conspiracy to defraud.

An example would be where two or more people agree to temporarily deprive another of his property. Since there is no intention to permanently deprive the victim of property, this would not amount to an agreement to steal contrary to s 1 of the Theft Act 1968, but could constitute a common law conspiracy to defraud.

It is not clear precisely what type of behaviour is required to amount to defrauding. In *Scott v MPC* (1975), Lord Diplock suggested that, where the intended victim was a private individual, the purpose of the conspirators must be to cause economic loss by interfering with some proprietary right. In the case of a public official, the conspiracy to defraud should be intended to cause him to act contrary to his duty.

However, in *Wai Yu-Tsang v R* (1991), the Privy Council cast doubt on the distinction between private individuals and public officials and further held that conspiracies to defraud are not limited to cases of intention to cause economic loss. It seems that all that is required is proof that the conspirators 'dishonestly agreed to bring about a state of affairs which they realise will or may deceive the victim'.

The *mens rea* for conspiracy to defraud requires proof of an intention to defraud and evidence of dishonesty. In *Wai Yu-Tsang v R* (1991), Lord Goff said that intent to defraud simply meant 'an intention to practise a fraud on another, or an intention to act to the prejudice of another man's right'.

It is suggested that where dishonesty is in issue the *Ghosh* test can be applied.

Conspiracy to corrupt public morals

This common law offence is preserved by s 5(3) of the Criminal Law Act 1977 because, following the decision of the House of Lords in *Shaw v DPP* (1962), there was some uncertainty as to whether or not there was a substantive offence of corrupting public morals. Although the better view, perhaps, is that there is not.

If there is, indeed, a substantive offence of corrupting public morals then an agreement to do this would amount to a statutory conspiracy and there would be no need for the common law offence. However, it can be argued that, if there is no such substantive offence, then the common law offence is necessary to impose liability on those who agree to bring this consequence about.

Conspiracy to outrage public decency

It is now well established that there is a substantive offence of outraging public decency (*Knuller v DPP* (1973); *R v Rowley* (1991); *R v Gibson and Another* (1991)). The retention of the common law offence of conspiring to outrage public decency is no longer necessary as this conduct would now amount to a statutory conspiracy.

Common law or statutory conspiracy?

According to s 12 of the Criminal Justice Act 1987, statutory conspiracy and common law conspiracy are not mutually exclusive. The prosecution can choose which offence to charge in cases of overlap.

Impossibility

Impossibility is no defence to a charge of statutory conspiracy (s 1(1)(b) of the Criminal Law Act 1977), but may be a defence to a common law conspiracy (*DPP v Nock* (1978)).

In order to constitute a defence to common law conspiracy, the impossibility must relate to something other than the means used to bring the offence about (*Haughton v Smith* (1975)).

Attempt

Definition
By s 1(1) of the Criminal Attempts Act 1981:

> If with intent to commit an offence to which this section applies, a person does an act which is more than merely preparatory to the commission of the offence, he is guilty of attempting to commit the offence.

Actus reus
It must be proved that the defendant has gone beyond mere preparation, although it is no longer necessary for the 'last act' prior to the commission of the offence to have been committed (*R v Gullefer* (1987)).

Lord Lane in *Gullefer* said that the 1981 Act sought to steer a 'midway course' between mere preparation, on the one hand, and the 'last act' necessary to commit the offence on the other. He went on to state that the attempt begins 'when the defendant embarks on the crime proper'.

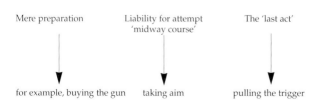

It seems that the courts take a relatively restricted view of what amounts to going beyond mere preparation. For example, in *R v Campbell* (1991), the defendant, who was armed with an imitation firearm, was arrested within a yard of the door of a post office which he intended to rob. Nevertheless, the Court of Appeal held that there was no evidence on which a jury could 'properly and safely' find that the defendant's acts were more than merely preparatory. Similarly, in *Geddes* (1996), the defendant was found in the boys' toilet of a school, equipped with lengths of string, sealing tape and a knife. He was charged and convicted of attempted false imprisonment, but successfully appealed. Although there was no doubt about the defendant's intention, it was held that the evidence showed no more than that he had made preparations, got himself ready and positioned himself ready to commit the offence. He had not had any contact with any potential victim, nor could it be said that he had moved from the role of preparation and planning into the area of execution or implementation. In short, there was no evidence that he did anything more than merely preparatory actions.

In *Tosti* (1977), the two accused had provided themselves with oxyacetylene equipment, driven to the scene of a planned burglary, concealed the equipment in a hedge, approached the door of a barn and examined the padlock on it. They then became aware that they were being watched and ran off. They were convicted of attempted burglary and their subsequent appeal was dismissed.

The distinction between *Geddes* and *Tosti* is that, in the former case, the evidence did not show that the defendant had made contact with a victim (that is, a child to imprison), whereas, in the latter, the accused had made contact with a target (that is, the barn to burgle). Presumably, it was when the accused started to 'examine' the padlock that they moved beyond planning and preparation to execution.

The judge decides whether there is sufficient evidence to put to the jury, but it is the jury who must decide whether the defendant's acts have gone beyond mere preparation and thus come within the s 1(1) definition of an attempt (*R v Griffin* (1993) and see s 4(3) of the Criminal Attempts Act 1981).

Mens rea

The defendant must have the intention to commit the offence in question (*Mohan v R* (1976)). Following the decision in *R v Walker and Hayles* (1990), it appears that indirect intent will suffice.

Where an offence requires *mens rea* as to a circumstance, such as recklessness as to whether the victim of rape consents to intercourse, then the prosecution will have to prove intention as to the central conduct (that is, intercourse) and recklessness (of the *Cunningham* type) as to consent (*R v Khan* (1990) and *AG's Reference (No 3 of 1992)* (1994)).

Impossibility

It is now clear that impossibility, whether factual or legal, will be no defence to a charge of attempt (*R v Shivpuri* (1986)).

Offences that can be attempted

Generally, any offence triable in England and Wales as an indictable offence (that is, any offence triable only on indictment, or triable either way) may be attempted (s 1(4) of the Criminal Attempts Act 1981).

However, the following offences cannot be attempted:

- statutory or common law conspiracy;

- offences of assisting an arrestable offender or compounding an arrestable offence contrary to s 4(1) and s 5(1) of the Criminal Law Act 1967;
- aiding, abetting, counselling or procuring the commission of an offence (s 1(4)(b) of the Criminal Attempts Act 1981).

Where aiding, etc, is the principal offence as in s 2(1) of the Suicide Act 1961, an attempt to aid is an offence because this would not amount to aiding an offence within the terms of s 1(4)(b) of the Criminal Attempts Act 1981.

Conditional intention

Where a person takes a bag with the intention of stealing the contents if there are any and if they are valuable, it might be argued that he has only a conditional intention to steal the contents and that such an unconditional intention is insufficient for the offence of both attempted theft and theft itself. The problem of conditional intention was considered by the courts in cases such as *Easom* (1971); *Huneyn* (1977); and *AG's References (Nos 1 and 2 of 1979)* (1979). However, it would appear that the effect of the Criminal Attempts Act 1981 as interpreted by the House of Lords in *Shivpuri* (1986) is that a defendant can now be convicted of attempting to steal property which he believed to be in existence, or of value.

Participation

The principal

The principal is the person whose act is the most immediate cause of the *actus reus* of the crime in question.

In murder, the principal is the person who, with *mens rea*, fires the fatal shot. In theft, it is the person who dishonestly appropriates property belonging to another with an intention to permanently deprive the other of it.

The accomplice
An accomplice is someone who has helped or encouraged the principal offender to commit the crime.

Joint principals
In some cases, it will be impossible to distinguish between principals and accomplices, for example, where two or more defendants stab the victim intending to murder him and the combined effect of the wounds does kill him. In these circumstances, the defendants could be charged as joint principals.

The test for distinguishing between a joint principal and an accomplice would seem to be to ask whether the defendant by his own actions, as distinct from anything done by the other parties to the crime, contributed to the causation of the *actus reus*. If the answer is 'yes', then the defendant is a joint principal rather than an accomplice.

Joint enterprise
A new basis for criminal liability has appeared in the Law Commission's Consultation Paper No 131, *Assisting and Encouraging Crime*, and, in the case of *Stewart and Schofield* (1995), where Hobhouse LJ said:

> The allegation that a defendant took part in the execution of a crime as joint enterprise is not the same as an allegation that he aided, abetted, counselled or procured the commission of that crime. A person who is a mere aider or abettor, etc, is truly a secondary party to the commission of whatever crime it is that the principal has committed although he may be charged

as a principal. If the principal has committed the crime of murder, the liability of the secondary party can only be a liability for aiding and abetting murder. In contrast, where the allegation is joint enterprise, the allegation is that one defendant participated in the criminal act of another. This is a different principle.

This new joint enterprise doctrine focuses on participation during the commission of the offence, whereas traditional accessorial liability encompasses assistance or encouragement before the commission of the offence.

It is difficult to see the difference as far as the *actus reus* is concerned between joint enterprise and traditional accessorial liability. How can a defendant 'participate' in the criminal act of another except by assisting or encouraging him, that is, aiding, abetting, counselling or procuring?

As far as the *mens rea* is concerned, that required of an accessory is an intention to assist or encourage the commission of the offence combined with knowledge of the type of offence which the principal commits (*R v Bainbridge* (1959)). The decision in *Hyde* (1991) is important on the imposition of joint liability. Lord Lane held that, if a defendant realised (without agreeing to such conduct) that the principal might kill or cause grievous bodily harm, but nevertheless continued to participate in the venture, then that would amount to sufficient *mens rea* for secondary liability for murder.

However, in *R v Wan and Chan* (1995), it was held that where two people agree to assault another and in the course of the assault one of them causes grievous bodily harm and intends to do so, the other is not guilty of the more serious offence if he did not himself intend to cause grievous bodily harm since the principal would have deliberately gone beyond the scope of what the defendants had agreed to do. It seems that the court assumed that the joint enterprise principles, discussed above, were also relevant to an individual who counselled or procured the commission of an offence, but is absent when the offence is committed, just as they apply to an aider or abettor present at the scene of the crime.

Unfortunately, the House of Lords in *R v Powell* (1997), far from resolving the complexities noted above, appears to have introduced a further complicating factor. The House held that it is sufficient to found a conviction for murder for a secondary party to have realised that, in the course of the joint enterprise, the principal might kill with intent to do so or with intent to cause grievous bodily harm.

At first sight, it appears that this decision does no more than confirm the decision in *Hyde*. However, probably without the House realising it, the case has added a new element; the accomplice must now foresee not only that the principal might kill or cause grievous bodily harm, but also that the principal might do so with an intention to kill or cause grievous bodily harm. Unfortunately, this aspect of the decision in *Powell* does not seem altogether compatible with the principle, previously established by the House of Lords, that a secondary party can be liable for a more serious offence than the principal one (*R v Howe* (1987); see also *Uddin* (1998) and *Greatrex* (1998)).

Innocent agency
If the *actus reus* of the crime in question has been brought about by the action of someone who has no *mens rea*, or who has a defence such as automatism, insanity or infancy, then that person can be termed an innocent agent.

In these circumstances, the principal is the person whose act is the most immediate cause of the innocent agent's act. For example, if A hypnotises B and commands him to perform the *actus reus* of an offence while he is in an hypnotic trance, it is A who is the principal and B the innocent agent.

Definition

Section 8 of the Accessories and Abettors Act 1861, as amended, provides:

> Whosoever, shall aid, abet, counsel, or procure the commission of any misdemeanour ... shall be liable to be tried, indicted and punished as a principal offender.

It can be seen from the above definition that the *actus reus* of secondary liability can take the form of one or more of the following modes of participation.

ACTION	TIME	CAUSATION REQUIRED?	CONSENSUS REQUIRED?
Aiding, that is, helping	Before or during offence	Yes (1)	No
Abetting, that is, encouraging	During offence	No	Yes
Counselling, that is, encouraging or threatening	Before offence	Yes (2)	Yes
Procuring, that is, causing	Before	Yes (3)	No

(1) Causation is required in the sense that the defendant must assist the principal to commit the offence earlier, more easily or more safely.

(2) Counselling must have had some effect on the defendant's mind.

(3) Direct causation required.

Modes of participation

An exception
If the defendant is under a legal duty (for example, a contractual duty) to aid the principal, for example, by returning property which the principal owns, he will not be liable as an accomplice even though he knows the type of offence which the principal intends to commit (*R v Lomas* (1913)).

Mere presence at the scene of the crime
Mere presence at the scene of the crime will not be sufficient to amount to any of the above modes of participation (*R v Coney* (1882); *R v Clarkson* (1971)).

Obviously, abetting or counselling will occur where a spectator applauds or purchases a ticket for an illegal performance (*Wilcox v Jeffery* (1951)).

Mens rea
The requisite *mens rea* consists of an *intention* to aid, abet, etc, and *knowledge* of the type of crime the principal intends to commit (*R v Bainbridge* (1960)).

In relation to murder, it must be proved that the accomplice foresaw death or grievous bodily harm as a *possible* incident of the planned offence being carried out (*R v Hyde* (1991)).

The 'blank cheque' rule
Where the defendant has given the principal assistance or encouragement to commit one of a range of offences, in short, a 'blank cheque' to offend, then the accomplice will be liable for any offence that the principal actually commits within that range of contemplated offences (*Maxwell v DPP for Northern Ireland* (1979)).

Acts within the scope of the common plan

If, as a result of carrying out a common plan, the defendant contributes towards the causation of the *actus reus* of an offence, he would incur liability as a joint principal.

Similarly, the defendant will incur liability as an accomplice if the principal commits any offence within the scope of those contemplated.

Accidental departure from the common plan

The general rule is that an accomplice will be liable for all accidental, or unforeseen consequences that flow from the common plan being carried out (*R v Baldessare* (1930)).

Deliberate departure from the common plan

Where the principal deliberately departs from the common plan, the other parties will not be liable in respect of any consequences of his action (*Davies v DPP* (1954); *R v English* (1997)).

Withdrawal from the common plan

What will amount to an effective withdrawal will depend upon which mode of participation the accomplice has engaged in. If the defendant has assisted or encouraged the commission of the offence prior to its commission, then it seems that all that is required is that the defendant clearly communicates his withdrawal from the common plan (*R v Grundy* (1977); *R v Rook* (1993)).

Where the defendant aids or abets at the scene of the crime, then much more will be required in order to constitute an effective withdrawal. Indeed, in these circumstances, nothing less than physical intervention may be required (*R v Becerra and Cooper* (1975)). However, in the case of spontaneous, as opposed to pre-planned violence, a participant can effectively withdraw from the joint enterprise without necessarily communicating that withdrawal to the other parties (*R v Mitchell* (1998)).

Victims as accomplices

In *R v Tyrrell* (1894), a girl below the age of 16 was found not guilty of aiding and abetting a man to have unlawful sexual intercourse with her. The principle was that a defendant cannot incur liability as an accomplice if the offence in question is one that was designed to protect a class of people of which the defendant is a member.

Acquittal of the principal

If the principal is acquitted because he has not committed the *actus reus* of the offence in question, then the defendant will not be liable as an accomplice as there is no offence to assist or encourage (*Thornton v Mitchell* (1940)). However, even if the principal has not committed the *actus reus* of the full offence, he may still be liable for attempt. In these circumstances, the defendant could be liable for aiding and abetting the attempt.

If the principal is acquitted because he can avail himself of some defence which is not available to the defendant, there is nothing to prevent the conviction of the defendant as an accomplice (*R v Bourne* (1952)).

If the principal is acquitted because he lacks the *mens rea* or capacity for the crime in question, the defendant may still incur liability either as a principal who has acted through an innocent agent (*R v Michael* (1840)) or as an accomplice (*R v Cogan and Leak* (1975); *DPP v K and C* (1997)).

	Accomplice Liable?	
	Yes	No
Principal lacks *actus reus*		✔
Principal lacks *mens rea*	✔	
Principal lacks capacity	✔	
Principal has defence not available to accomplice	✔	
Accomplice is a victim		✔

3 Non-fatal offences against the person

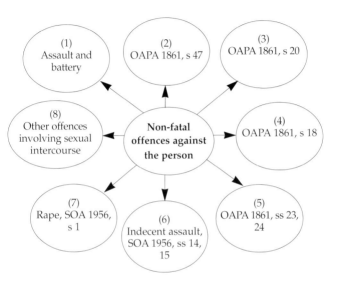

(1) Assault and battery

Actus reus

The *actus reus* of an assault consists of causing the victim to apprehend immediate physical violence (*Logden v DPP* (1976)).

For many years, it was uncertain whether words alone could constitute an assault (*R v Meade and Belt* (1823); *R v Wilson* (1955)). However, it seems settled that words can negate an assault (*Tuberville v Savage* (1669)). Moreover, in *R v Burstow; R v Ireland* (1997), the House of Lords held that an assault could be committed by words alone, thus ending this long standing uncertainty. The emphasis is now on the effect of the defendant's actions on the victim, rather than the means adopted by the defendant.

The *actus reus* of a battery consists of the actual infliction of unlawful physical violence. The degree of 'violence' required is minimal and can consist of the least touching of another (*Cole v Turner* (1705)).

Touching a person's clothing will amount to a battery, provided the contact is both unauthorised and capable of being felt by the victim (*R v Thomas* (1985)).

The courts presume that people impliedly consent to the normal touching that occurs in everyday life (*Collins v Wilcock* (1984)).

A battery can be inflicted indirectly, for example, by setting a trap for the victim (*DPP v K* (1990)).

Mens rea

The *mens rea* for both assault and battery is intention or recklessness in the *Cunningham* sense.

Statutory offences

The Divisional Court in *DPP v Little* (1991) found that not only were common assault and battery separate offences, but also that the Offences Against the Person Act 1861 had put them into a statutory form. It is, therefore, no longer correct to refer to them as common law assault and battery. They should now be charged under s 39 of the Criminal Justice Act 1988.

(2) Section 47 of the Offences Against the Person Act 1861

Definition

Section 47 of the Offences Against the Person Act 1861 provides that it is an offence to commit 'any assault occasioning actual bodily harm'.

Actus reus

An 'assault' within the meaning of s 47 can consist of either an assault in the technical sense of causing someone to fear immediate unlawful violence, or in the sense of a battery (that is, the infliction of unlawful violence).

'Occasioning' means the same as 'causing', therefore, the rules relating to causation will be relevant. It will be remembered that the main test for establishing causation in law is to ask whether the result was a reasonably foreseeable consequence of what the defendant was doing. However, in *R v Roberts* (1971), Stephenson LJ said that only if the actions of the victim could be shown to be 'daft' would the chain of causation be broken. It is sometimes argued that this *dictum* conflicts with the 'thin skull' rule that the defendant must take his victim as he finds him.

Actual bodily harm was defined in *R v Miller* (1954) so as to include any hurt or injury likely to interfere with the health or comfort of the victim. In *R v Chan-Fook* (1993), it was held that actual bodily harm includes psychiatric injury, but does not include mere emotions such as fear, distress or panic. The House of Lords, in *Burstow and Ireland* (1997), confirmed the decision in *Chan-Fook* by holding that recognisable psychiatric illness can amount to 'bodily harm' for the purposes of ss 47, 20 and 18 of the Offences Against the Person Act 1861. In *R v Morris* (1997), the Court of Appeal held that, when on a charge of an assault occasioning actual bodily harm and the harm is alleged to have been occasioned by a non-physical assault, the case should not go to the jury without expert psychiatric evidence.

Mens rea

The *mens rea* is intention or recklessness of the *Cunningham* type. Either of these two mental states need to be established only in relation to the initial assault; it is unnecessary to prove that the defendant intended or foresaw the risk of harm, however slight (*R v Savage* (1991)).

(3) Section 20 of the Offences Against the Person Act 1861

Definition

Section 20 of the Offences Against the Person Act 1861 creates two offences of 'malicious wounding' and 'maliciously inflicting grievous bodily harm'.

Actus reus

A wounding requires a complete break of all the layers of the victim's skin (*JCC v Eisenhower* (1984)). Grievous bodily harm simply means 'serious harm' (*R v Saunders* (1985)).

Although most offences under s 20 will involve an assault, it was decided in *R v Wilson* (1983) that 'inflicting' does not necessarily imply an assault. It would seem that if 'inflicting' is to have any meaning at all it is to imply the need for causation (see also *R v Burstow* (1997)).

Mens rea

The word 'malicious' implies a *mens rea* of intention or recklessness of the *Cunningham* type.

The decision of the court in *Mowatt* (1967) placed a 'gloss' on the *Cunningham* definition of recklessness in relation to s 20 in that the defendant must be shown to have been aware of the possibility of causing the victim *some physical harm*, albeit not serious harm.

It follows that foresight that the victim will be frightened is insufficient to found liability in relation to s 20; as stated above, the defendant must have foreseen some physical harm, if only of a minor character (*R v Sullivan* (1981)).

An intention to inflict a wound, not amounting to serious harm, would constitute sufficient *mens rea* for the s 20 offence, but not for the s 18 offence (see below).

(4) Section 18 of the Offences Against the Person Act 1861

Definition

By s 18 of the Offences Against the Person Act 1861, it is an offence to 'maliciously ... wound or cause any grievous bodily harm ... with intent to do some grievous bodily harm'.

Actus reus

The *actus reus* for this offence is exactly the same as that for the s 20 offence and consists of either a wound or grievous bodily harm.

Mens rea

A specific intent to cause grievous bodily harm is required for this offence (*R v Belfon* (1976)).

Summary of non-sexual offences

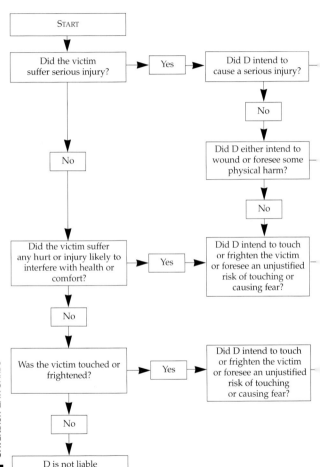

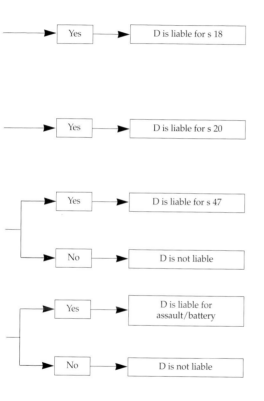

(5) Sections 23 and 24 of the Offences Against the Person Act 1861

Actus reus
Both ss 23 and 24 require the administration of a noxious substance. Whether or not a substance is noxious will depend upon the circumstances in which it is taken. Such circumstances include the quality and quantity of the substance as well as the characteristics of the person to whom it is given (*R v Marcus* (1981)).

'Administering' means causing to be taken, for example, by spraying CS gas into someone's face (*R v Gillard* (1988)).

The *actus reus* of s 23 requires that life must be endangered or grievous bodily harm inflicted as a consequence of the administration of the noxious substance.

Mens rea
Both offences require that the noxious substance be administered intentionally or recklessly in the *Cunningham* sense.

In addition, s 24 requires proof of a further intent to injure, aggrieve or annoy the victim.

(6) Indecent assault

Actus reus
The offence requires proof of an assault in circumstances of indecency. Indecent assault on a woman is charged contrary to s 14 of the Sexual Offences Act 1956. Indecent assault on a man is charged contrary to s 15. A girl or boy under the age of 16 cannot in law give any consent that would prevent an act being an assault for the purposes of ss 14 and 15. Most

indecent assaults involve physical contact, but an indecent assault where the defendant does not touch the victim is possible, if the victim is shown to have apprehended immediate physical violence (*R v Sargeant* (1997)).

Indecency involves conduct that contravenes standards of decent behaviour in regard to sexual modesty or privacy (*R v Court* (1989)). It does not encompass conduct that is, objectively, incapable of being indecent – such as removing a woman's shoe (*R v George* (1956)). Where the defendant's conduct is ambiguous (that is, it could be regarded as being indecent) evidence of the purpose with which he acted can be put before the jury to help them determine the issue (*R v Court* (1989)).

Mens rea
The defendant must have an intention to assault or at least be '*Cunningham*' reckless as to whether or not the victim will be assaulted. Lord Ackner in *R v Court* stated that for the defendant to be liable to be convicted of indecent assault, where the circumstances of the alleged offence can be given an innocent as well as an indecent interpretation, the prosecution would have to prove that he intended to commit both an assault and an indecent one (that is, the defendant must be shown to have had an awareness of the indecency).

Consent to indecent assault
Consent is a defence to indecent assault provided the victim is capable of validly giving consent. A victim under the age of 16 or intoxicated by drugs cannot validly consent. A defendant, who honestly believes that the victim is

consenting to the activity, and who honestly believes that the victim has the capacity to consent, will not be guilty of indecent assault. This includes situations where the defendant honestly believes that the victim (who is in fact under 16, but who is consenting), is over the age of 16 (*R v K* (2001)).

If the victim is deceived as to the nature or quality of the activity to which he or she appears to be consenting the consent given will not be valid (*R v Tabassum* (2000)).

(7) Rape

The offence of rape is based on s 1 of the Sexual Offences Act 1956 as amended by the Sexual Offences (Amendment) Act 1976, and s 142 of the Criminal Justice and Public Order Act 1994.

Actus reus

The offence of rape can only be committed by a man (a male above the age of 10) as a principal offender (a woman can be an accomplice to rape). The victim can be a man or a woman. It is an offence for a man to rape a woman or another man. Sexual intercourse is established by evidence of penile penetration of either vagina or anus. There is no need to prove ejaculation.

Unlike those offences to which consent can be raised as a defence, rape requires the prosecution to prove the absence of consent as part of the *actus reus* of the offence. The significance of this is that the absence of consent has to be established beyond all reasonable doubt.

In directing a jury as to whether or not a victim consented to sexual intercourse, Dunn LJ in *R v Olugboja* (1981) observed that:

The jury ... should be directed that consent, or the absence of it, is to be given its ordinary meaning and if need be, by way of example, that there is a difference between consent and submission; every consent involves a submission, but it by no means follows that a mere submission involves consent ... [I]n the ... type of case where intercourse takes place after threats not involving violence or the fear of it ... we think that ... a jury will have to be ... directed to concentrate on the state of mind of the victim immediately before the act of sexual intercourse, having regard to ... their combined good sense, experience and knowledge of human nature and modern behaviour to all the relevant facts of that case.

There will be no consent if:

- the victim laid down a precondition to intercourse that the defendant failed to comply with (*AG's Reference (No 28 of 1996)* (1997));

- the defendant impersonated the victim's husband – s 1(3) of the Sexual Offences Act 1956 – or partner (*R v Elbekkay* (1995));

- the defendant obtained the victim's consent by fraud (*R v Williams* (1923)).

Mens rea

The defendant must intend to have sexual intercourse. He must know that the victim is not consenting or must at least be '*Cunningham*' reckless as to whether or not the victim is consenting. The defendant is to be judged on the facts as he honestly believed them to be. His belief in the victim's consent does not have to be reasonable (*R v Morgan* (1975)). The less reasonable the defendant's belief that the victim was consenting, the less likely the jury are to believe him – s 1(2) of the Sexual Offences (Amendment) Act 1976. The recklessness as to whether or not the victim is consenting must be *'Cunningham'* recklessness (*R v Satnam; R v Kewal* (1983)).

(8) Other offences involving sexual intercourse

It is an offence for a man to have unlawful sexual intercourse with a girl under the age of 13 (s 5 of the Sexual Offences Act 1956), or under the age of 16 (s 6 of the Sexual Offences Act 1956). The offence under s 5 is one of strict liability, in that a defendant cannot rely on a mistake as to the victim's age to escape liability. Under the less serious s 6 offence Parliament has provided for the so called 'young man's defence'. If a defendant under the age of 24 honestly and reasonably believed that the girl was over the age of 16, and he has not previously been charged with a 'like offence' he may have a defence.

If the defendant induces a victim below the age of 18 to consent to sexual intercourse or other sexual activity by abusing a position of trust he may commit an offence contrary to s 3 of the Sexual Offences (Amendment) Act 2000. For these purposes 'sexual activity' is further defined by s 3(5) as excluding any activity which a reasonable person would regard as sexual only with knowledge of the intentions, motives or feelings of the parties; but otherwise including any activity that a reasonable person would regard as sexual in all the circumstances.

4 Fatal offences

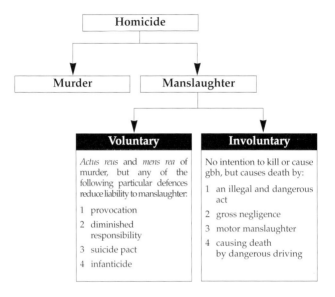

Murder

Actus reus

The *actus reus* of murder is causing the death of a human being.

A patient kept alive on a life support machine is not regarded as legally dead and is, therefore, capable of being murdered. The original attacker will be held to have caused death if the machine is turned off as a result of a medical decision made in good faith (*R v Malcherek and Steel* (1981)).

The law of homicide protects the newborn child once it becomes capable of independent existence from the mother. There is no need for the umbilical cord to have been cut (*R v Reeves* (1839)), but the child must have been totally expelled from the mother's womb (*R v Poulton* (1832)).

Mens rea

The necessary *mens rea* for murder is an intention to kill or cause grievous bodily harm (*R v Vickers* (1957)).

In cases where it is not clear whether the defendant had such an intention, the jury must consider the evidence of what the defendant actually foresaw, and the more evidence there is that he foresaw death or grievous bodily harm as a consequence of his actions, then the stronger the inference that he intended to kill (*R v Hancock and Shankland* (1986)).

In *R v Nedrick* (1986), the court supplemented the decision in *Hancock* by suggesting that the jury must be satisfied that the defendant foresaw death or grievous bodily harm as a virtual certainty before they could infer intention. The House of Lords, in *R v Woollin* (1998), confirmed the approach of the Court of Appeal in *Nedrick*.

Manslaughter

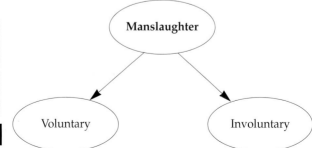

Voluntary manslaughter

There are four particular defences that can operate to reduce a charge of murder to that of manslaughter: provocation, diminished responsibility, suicide pact and infanticide.

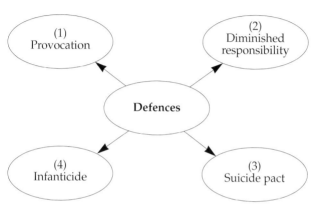

(1) Provocation

The basis for the defence

At common law provocation was defined by Devlin J in *R v Duffy* (1949) as:

... some act or series of acts done by the dead man to the accused which would cause in any reasonable person and actually causes in the accused, a sudden and temporary loss of self-control, rendering the accused so subject to passion as to make him for the moment not master of his mind.

Section 3 of the Homicide Act 1957 expanded upon this by providing that:

> Where on a charge of murder there is evidence on which the jury can find that the person charged was provoked (whether by things done or by things said or by both together) to lose his self-control, the question whether the provocation was enough to make a reasonable man do as he did shall be left to be determined by the jury; and in determining that question the jury shall take into account everything both done and said according to the effect which, in their opinion, it would have on a reasonable man.

Establishing provocation involves a two-stage process: first was the defendant provoked?; secondly whether the defendant satisfied the objective test in respect of the degree of self-control that he displayed.

Was the defendant provoked?
- There is no legal restriction on what can cause the provocation (*R v Doughty* (1986)).

- The provocation may be cumulative, the jury should be directed to consider the background to the case, including the history of the relationship between the defendant and the victim.

- The jury will be directed to distinguish between provocation and revenge. This may be indicated by the gap in time between the provocation and the killing. There is no set time limit. The question in every case must be whether, at the time of the killing, the defendant was acting under the effect of the provocation (*R v Ibrams and Gregory* (1981)).

The objective test

The House of Lords' decision in *DPP v Camplin* (1978) was thought to have laid down a reasonable person test for provocation – the defence only being made out where the defendant had shown the self-control to be expected of a reasonable person. The objective nature of this test was relaxed to the extent that the defendant's age and gender would be taken into account. Other characteristics, such as deformity, shameful past, sexual proclivities, ethnic origin, addictions etc would only be taken into account for the purposes of assessing the gravity of the provocation.

A number of subsequent Court of Appeal decisions indicated a further relaxation of the objective test as regards the self-control aspect of *Camplin* – the courts being willing to take into account characteristics such as having a mental age of 9 (*R v Raven* (1982)), battered woman syndrome (*R v Ahluwalia* (1992)), obsessive personality (*R v Dryden* (1995)), and dyslexia, anorexia and a tendency to attention-seeking by wrist-slashing (*R v Humphreys* (1995)).

These Court of appeal decisions were doubted by the Privy Council in *Luc Thiet Thuan v The Queen* (1996), but the approach of the Court of Appeal has since been confirmed as correct by the majority in the House of Lords' decision in *R v Smith (Morgan)* (2000).

In applying the objective stage of the test for provocation the courts should no longer distinguish between characteristics that are relevant for the purposes of determining whether or not the defendant exercised the self-control to be expected of a reasonable man, and characteristics relevant to determining the gravity of the provocation. The concept of the reasonable person has effectively disappeared. The jury should now ask whether the defendant displayed the degree of self-control that it was fair and just to expect from *him*, bearing in mind that certain character traits, such as male possessiveness, jealousy, a tendency to violent rages or childish tantrums, pugnacity and irritability were not to be seen as excuses for engaging in violent acts.

(2) Diminished responsibility

Section 2(1) of the Homicide Act 1957 provides:

> Where a person kills or is a party to the killing of another, he shall not be convicted of murder if he was suffering from such abnormality of mind (whether arising from a condition of arrested or retarded development of mind or any inherent causes or induced by disease or injury) as subsequently impaired his mental responsibility for his acts and omissions in doing or being a party to the killing.

In *R v Byrne* (1960), Lord Parker CJ defined abnormality of mind as 'a state of mind that the reasonable person would find abnormal'. Where the jury has to deal with both diminished responsibility and intoxication, they should first consider whether the defendant would have killed as he did, even if he had not been intoxicated. If the answer is 'yes', then, they should go on to consider whether he would have been suffering from diminished responsibility when he did so (*R v Atkinson* (1985)).

However, where it is alleged that the defendant was suffering from diminished responsibility caused by the disease of alcoholism (as opposed to mere intoxication), the jury must try to establish whether the first drink was taken voluntarily – if so, the defence will fail (*R v Tandy* (1989); *R v Egan* (1992)).

(3) Suicide pact

Section 4 of the Homicide Act 1957 provides that any killing carried out in pursuance of a suicide pact will be treated as manslaughter, rather than as murder.

(4) Infanticide

Section 1(1) of the Infanticide Act 1938 provides that, where a woman kills her child before it reaches the age of 12 months and there is evidence to show that at the time of the killing the balance of her mind was disturbed by the effect of giving birth, then the jury is entitled to find her guilty of infanticide rather than murder.

Involuntary manslaughter

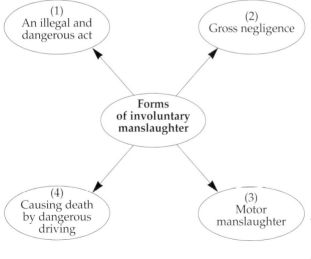

(1) Constructive manslaughter

This offence requires proof that the defendant intentionally committed a dangerous criminal act which resulted in the death of the victim.

The objective nature of the 'dangerous' act was established in *R v Church* (1966), where it was said that:

> ... the unlawful act must be such as all sober and reasonable people would inevitably recognise must subject the other person to, at least, the risk of some harm ...

What is meant by 'harm' in this context was clarified in *R v Dawson* (1985) where it was held that the jury must be directed to consider the possibility of *physical* harm as opposed to mere emotional disturbance.

Moreover, the reasonable person should be endowed with all the knowledge that the defendant has gained in the course of the crime (*R v Watson* (1989)).

The illegal act required for constructive manslaughter must be a criminal act (*R v Franklin* (1883)), but there is no need for the act to be 'aimed' at the victim in the sense of being intended to do him some harm (*R v Goodfellow* (1986)).

In *R v Kennedy* (1999), the Court of Appeal held that a defendant who injected himself with heroin had committed an unlawful act.

It follows that any act which is both dangerous and criminal will be capable of forming the *actus reus* of the offence. All that is required for the *mens rea* is an intention to do such an act; it is not necessary for the defendant to know that the act is criminal or dangerous (*DPP v Newbury and Jones* (1976)).

(2) Killing by gross negligence

Following the decision of the House of Lords in *R v Adomako* (1994), to establish this form of manslaughter the prosecution must prove:

- A duty of care
  It is submitted that the concept of a duty of care, obviously borrowed from the law of tort, is unlikely to prove problematic in the context of criminal law. Surely there is a general duty to take care not to engage in anti-social behaviour?

- Breach of that duty
  The duty not to behave in an anti-social way will be breached whenever there is a reasonably foreseeable risk of injury to health (as opposed to the risk of physical injury required for motor manslaughter) occurring (*R v Stone and Dobinson* (1977)).

- Gross negligence
  According to the Court of Appeal in *R v Prentice and Others* (1993), a decision confirmed by the House of Lords in *R v Adomako*, any of the following states of mind could lead a jury to make a finding of gross negligence:

  (a) indifference to an obvious risk of injury to health;

  (b) actual foresight of the risk coupled with the determination nevertheless to run it;

  (c) an appreciation of the risk coupled with an intention to avoid it but also coupled with such a high degree of negligence in the attempted avoidance as the jury considers justifies conviction;

  (d) inattention or failure to advert to a serious risk which goes beyond 'mere inadvertence' in respect of an obvious and important matter which the defendant's duty demanded he should address.

Two of the above four types of gross negligence, (a) and (b), seem to be subjective mental states (in relation to (a), surely, you can only be *indifferent* to a result which is foreseen?), whereas (c) and (d) are clearly objective mental states. However, each case, it seems, is subject to the overriding judgment of the jury: '... gross negligence which the jury consider justifies criminal conviction ...'

In *R v Watts* (1998), the Court of Appeal held that, when directing a jury in a case of alleged manslaughter by gross negligence, the judge should follow the approach laid down in *Prentice* and confirmed by *Adomako*.

It should be noted that, in *R v Khan (Rungzahe) and Khan (Tabir)* (1998), the Court of Appeal held that there is no separate category of manslaughter called manslaughter by omission. For a killing to amount to manslaughter, the omission must amount to a breach of duty by the defendant and the facts must satisfy the requirements of constructive manslaughter or manslaughter by gross negligence.

A company can be convicted of corporate manslaughter based on killing by gross negligence but only where there is evidence establishing the guilty mind of an identified human individual for the same crime – that individual must be an employee senior enough to be regarded as the directing mind and will of the company (*AG's Reference (No 2 of 1999)* (2000)).

(3) Motor manslaughter

The *actus reus* of this common law offence consists of driving in such a manner as to cause the death of another road user.

In *Adomako*, the House of Lords, overruling the earlier decision of the House in *R v Seymour* (1983), held that gross negligence was the proper *mens rea* for this offence. Lord Mackay stated that motor manslaughter charges should be reserved not only for the most culpable instances of negligence, but also for cases where the breach of duty brought with it a risk, not merely of injury or damage (as with the statutory offence – see below), but of death. It seems that, for manslaughter involving motor vehicles, what is required is driving so far below that of the reasonable driver as to be not only dangerous, but *inherently life threatening*.

(4) *Causing death by dangerous driving*

Causing death by dangerous driving, defined in s 1 and s 2A of the Road Traffic Act 1988, as substituted by s 1 of the Road Traffic Act 1991, is, in effect, causing death by grossly negligent driving.

This is because the defendant's driving must fall *far below* the standard of the reasonably competent driver.

It must be obvious to the careful and competent driver that driving in the way that the defendant was actually driving would cause danger of injury to the person or serious damage to property.

Summary

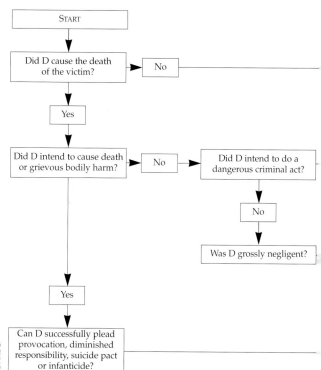

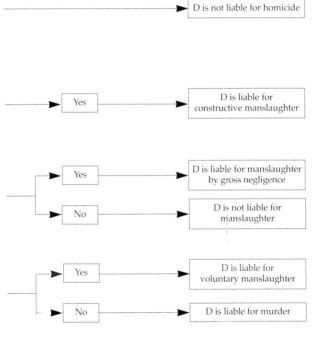

5 Offences against property

(1) Theft

Definition

The basic definition of theft is to be found in s 1(1) of the Theft Act 1968 which provides that a person who:

... dishonestly appropriates property belonging to another with the intention of permanently depriving the other of it ...

is guilty of theft.

Actus reus

Property

Section 4(1) of the Theft Act 1968 defines 'property' as:

> ... money and all other property, real or personal, including things in action and other intangible property.

This seemingly all encompassing definition is subject to both common law and statutory exceptions. The following do not constitute property:

- information (*Oxford v Moss* (1979));
- electricity (*Low v Blease* (1975));
- a human corpse (*R v Sharpe* (1857));
- land (s 4(2));
- wild plants (s 4(3));
- wild animals (s 4(4)).

However, there are also some exceptions to the exceptions rendering some of the above capable of being stolen in certain circumstances:

- a human corpse does become property capable of being stolen if skill or effort has been exercised on it (*Doodeward v Spence* (1907)); moreover, products of the body, such as blood and urine are capable of being stolen (*R v Rothery* (1976); *R v Welsh* (1974)). In *R v Kelly* (1998), the Court of Appeal held that human body parts are capable of being the subject of a charge of theft if they have acquired different attributes by virtue of the application of skill, such as dissection or preservation techniques;

- land can be appropriated by (a) a trustee, personal representative or liquidator; (b) someone not in possession can appropriate anything severed from the land; and (c) a tenant can appropriate any fixture (s 4(2)(a), (b) and (c));
- wild plants can be stolen if the whole plant is taken or the plant is taken for sale or reward (s 4(3));
- wild animals can be stolen if they are tamed or ordinarily kept in captivity or have been, or are in the process of being, reduced into another's possession (s 4(4)).

Belonging to another
The basic definition of 'belonging to another' is contained in s 5(1) of the Theft Act 1968:

> Property shall be regarded as belonging to any person having possession or control of it, or having in it any proprietary right or interest ...

Thus, in *R v Turner No 2* (1971), an owner was convicted of theft of his car when he removed it from a garage where it was undergoing repairs without informing the proprietor. Since the garage had possession and control, the car was treated as if it belonged to another in accordance with s 5(1).

The above case is often contrasted with that of *R v Meredith* (1973) where it was held that a car owner who had removed his vehicle from a police pound could not be guilty of appropriating his own property. As the police clearly had control of the car, the decision is difficult to reconcile with *Turner* and is, perhaps, best regarded as wrongly decided.

Section 5(3) of the Theft Act 1968 extends the meaning of 'belonging to another':

> Where a person receives property from or on account of another, and is under an obligation to the other to retain and deal with that property or its proceeds in a particular way, the property or proceeds shall be regarded (as against him) as belonging to another.

As the 'obligation' must be legally enforceable (*R v Gilks* (1972)), this will normally involve either contractual obligations or obligations imposed under a statute.

The terms of the contractual or statutory duty must be examined in order to establish the precise nature of the obligation. If the defendant is permitted to do what he likes with the property, his only obligation being to account in due course for an equivalent sum, s 5(3) does not apply (*R v Hall* (1973)). However, the defendant need not be under an obligation to retain particular monies; it is sufficient that he is under an obligation to keep in existence a fund equivalent to that which he has received (*Lewis v Lethbridge* (1987)).

It would appear that s 5(3) will apply where someone contracts on the basis that the money he hands over will be transferred by the recipient to a stakeholder or trustee. The recipient is under an obligation to deal with the money in a particular way and, if he dishonestly appropriates it, can be convicted of theft (*R v Kilneberg and Marsden* (1998)).

Section 5(4) covers the situation where the defendant receives property by mistake:

> Where a person gets property by another's mistake, and is under an obligation to make restitution ... then ... the property or proceeds shall be regarded (as against him) as belonging to the person entitled to restoration ...

If the mistake is fundamental, the sub-section is not of relevance as no property can pass under a void contract. Where the mistake is non-fundamental, the contract will be voidable, but, even in these circumstances, it can be argued that the sub-section is not relevant as there is no obligation to make restoration until the contract is actually avoided.

However, it seems that, in certain situations, the prosecution are able to argue that property belongs to another, either under a straightforward application of s 5(1), or via s 5(4):

- mistaken overpayment of wages (*AG's Reference (No 1 of 1983)* (1984));

- mistaken crediting of a bank account (*R v Shadrokh-Cigari* (1988)).

In addition, it is thought that the sub-section would apply to situations where the defendant receives too much change or too many goods by mistake.

Appropriation
Appropriation is defined in s 3(1) of the Theft Act 1968 as 'any assumption by a person or the rights of an owner'.

Appropriation can, therefore, take many forms, including:

- offering the property for sale (*R v Pitham and Hehl* (1976));

- taking the property;

- pledging the property;

- destroying (although not damaging) the property;

- fixing the price of the property (*R v Morris* (1983)).

In *R v Gomez* (1993), the House of Lords decided that any interference with property belonging to another would amount to an appropriation, irrespective of whether the owner consented or authorised the act in question.

As *Gomez* was a case where, on the facts, consent was obtained by fraud it was thought that its *ratio* could be restricted to such cases. This now seems doubtful in the light of *R v Hinks* (2000), where the House of Lords held that the defendant could be guilty of theft even though the property had been validly transferred to her in the form of a gift. The House of Lords brushed aside arguments that, if the transfer of property to the defendant was effected by means of a valid gift, the property could not be regarded as 'belonging to another'. The result is that everything depends on the defendant's state of mind, in particular whether or not the defendant is dishonest.

Mens rea

Dishonesty

There is a negative definition of dishonesty set out in s 2(1) of the Theft Act 1968. A person is not dishonest if he appropriates in the honest belief that:

- he has a legal right to deprive another of the property (s 2(1)(a));

- he would have the other's consent if the other knew of the appropriation and the circumstances of it (s 2(1)(b));

- the person to whom the property belongs cannot be discovered by taking reasonable steps (s 2(1)(c)).

A positive test for establishing dishonesty was laid down by the Court of Appeal in *R v Ghosh* (1982). In cases of doubt, the jury should be given the following direction:

Was the defendant dishonest according to the standards of ordinary decent people? If yes, did the defendant realise that what he was doing was dishonest by these standards?

Intention to permanently deprive

In the vast majority of cases, it will be obvious whether or not the defendant had an intention to permanently deprive the other of the property at the moment of appropriation. However, in two situations, the defendant will be deemed to have such an intention to permanently deprive:

- if it is his intention 'to treat the thing as his own to dispose of regardless of the other's rights: and a borrowing or lending of it may amount to so treating it if, but only if, the borrowing or lending is for a period and in circumstances making it equivalent to an outright taking or disposal' (s 6(1)); or

- where he parts with property 'under a condition as to its return which he may not be able to perform' (s 6(2)).

In relation to s 6(1), the intention to permanently deprive will be deemed to exist if the defendant intended to return the goods in a fundamentally changed state so that virtually all of their value would have been lost (*R v Lloyd* (1985)). Similarly, someone who deals with property knowing that he is doing so in a way which risks its loss may be intending to 'treat the thing as his own to dispose of regardless of the other's rights' and may, therefore, be deemed to have an intention to permanently deprive under s 6(1) (*R v Fernandes* (1995)).

In *R v Marshall, Coombes and Eren* (1998), it was held that someone who buys an Underground ticket from a passenger and who resells it would be guilty of theft by virtue of s 6(1).

(2) Robbery

Definition

Section 8(1) of the Theft Act 1968 provides that:

> A person is guilty of robbery if he steals and immediately before or at the time of doing so, and in order to do so, he uses force on any person or puts or seeks to put any person in fear of being then and there subjected to force.

Actus reus

Force

As can be seen from the above definition, the Act requires proof of either the use or the threat of force against the person. Whether force actually has been used or threatened is a matter for the jury to decide (*R v Dawson* (1976)).

The force can be used or threatened against any person, not necessarily the owner of the property (*Smith v Desmond Hall* (1965)).

It is clear that the force or threat of force must occur before or at the time of stealing. The use of force even seconds after the appropriation has taken place would not amount to robbery. However, the courts have been prepared on some occasions to hold that an appropriation could consist of a continuing act (*R v Hale* (1978)).

Stealing

All the elements required for s 1(1) theft are necessary to establish that the defendant has stolen for the purposes of robbery. Thus, in *R v Robinson* (1977), the defendant's conviction for robbery was quashed on the basis that, since he honestly believed that he was entitled to the property in question, he was not dishonest under s 2(1)(a) and, therefore, incapable of committing theft.

(3) Burglary

Definitions
Section 9 of the Theft Act 1968 creates two burglary offences.

Section 9(1)(a)
By s 9(1)(a), a person is guilty of burglary if 'he enters any building or part of a building as a trespasser' with an intention to:

- steal;
- inflict grievous bodily harm;
- rape;
- commit unlawful damage to the building or anything therein.

Section 9(1)(b)
A person is guilty of this offence if, having entered a building or part of a building as a trespasser, he steals or attempts to steal or inflict grievous bodily harm.

Actus reus
Both burglary offences require that the defendant has entered a building or part of a building as a trespasser.

Building or part of a building

There is no complete definition of what constitutes a 'building' contained in the Act. The following points should be noted in this respect:

- inhabited vehicles or vessels will amount to a 'building' for the purposes of the Act, even when the inhabiting person is not there;

- in *Stevens v Gourley* (1859), it was stated that a building was 'a structure of considerable size and intended to be permanent or at least to endure for a considerable length of time';

- in *B and S v Leathley* (1979), a large freezer container without wheels and which was connected to the electricity supply was held to constitute a building;

- in *Norfolk Constabulary v Seekings and Gould* (1986), a lorry trailer with wheels, used for storage and connected to the electricity supply, was not held to be a building;

- in *R v Walkington* (1979), a customer who went behind a till counter was held to enter part of a building as a trespasser.

Entry

Section 9 requires that the defendant must enter, or have entered, a building or part of a building. In *R v Collins* (1972), it was held that an entry must be 'effective and substantial'.

In *R v Brown* (1985), a case which involved the defendant leaning through a broken shop window, it was held that the crucial word in the *Collins* test was 'effective' and that 'substantial' did not materially assist in the matter. As the defendant was able to reach the articles he wished to steal, his entry was held to be 'effective' and the conviction was upheld.

Similarly, in *R v Ryan* (1995), a defendant who had his head and arm trapped inside a building by a window was held to have entered for the purposes of burglary. In the light of *Brown* and *Ryan,* it seems that the courts are adopting a very broad approach to the 'effective' and/or 'substantial' test established in *Collins*.

As a trespasser

The defendant must not only enter a building, he must do so as a trespasser. A trespasser is someone who enters property without express or implied permission.

A defendant who has permission to enter for particular purposes, but then exceeds the express or implied conditions of entry, will enter as a trespasser. For example, in *R v Smith and Jones* (1976), the defendants had permission to enter the house of Smith's father for normal domestic purposes, but not in order to steal the television set.

The defendant must know or be reckless in the *Cunningham* sense as to whether his entry is trespassory (*R v Collins* (1972)).

(4) Criminal damage

Definitions

Section 1(1)
This sub-section provides that the 'basic' offence of criminal damage is committed where:

> A person who without lawful excuse destroys or damages any property belonging to another, intending to destroy or damage any such property or being reckless as to whether any such property would be destroyed or damaged.

Section 1(2)

This sub-section states that an 'aggravated' offence is committed where:

> A person who without lawful excuse destroys or damages any property, whether belonging to himself or another:
>
> (a) intending to destroy or damage any property or being reckless as to whether any property would be destroyed or damaged; and
>
> (b) intending by the destruction or damage to endanger the life of another or being reckless as to whether the life of another would be thereby endangered.

Section 1(3)

This sub-section provides that where property is destroyed or damaged by fire, the offence is charged as arson and is punishable with a maximum sentence of life imprisonment.

Actus reus

Property

Property is defined in s 10(1) as anything of 'a tangible nature, whether real or personal, including money'.

Although somewhat similar to the definition of 'property' provided in s 4 of the Theft Act 1968, it should be noted that criminal damage can be committed in relation to land: while land cannot be stolen, conversely, intangible property can be stolen, but cannot be the subject of criminal damage.

Belonging to another

The property must belong to another for the purposes of s 1(1), but need not belong to another in relation to the s 1(2) offence.

Property will be treated as 'belonging to another' for the purposes of s 1(1) if that other has custody or control of it or has any proprietary right or interest in it or has a charge on it (s 10(2)).

Damage

Whether property has been destroyed or damaged will depend upon the circumstances of each case, the nature of the article and the way in which it is affected. The following cases provide illustrations of acts which were held to have amounted to criminal damage:

- in *Blake v DPP* (1993), a biblical quotation written on a concrete pillar with a marker pen was held to amount to criminal damage;

- similarly, in *Hardman and Others v Chief Constable of Avon and Somerset Constabulary* (1986), the spraying of human silhouettes by CND supporters on pavements was held to constitute criminal damage notwithstanding that the figures would be washed away by the next rainfall;

- in *Roe v Kingerlee* (1986), it was held that the application of mud to the walls of a cell could amount to damage as it would cost money to remove it;

- the unauthorised dumping of waste on a building site which cost £2,000 to remove was held to constitute criminal damage in *R v Henderson and Battley* (1984);

- in *Samuel v Stubbs* (1972), criminal damage was held to have been done to a policeman's helmet when it had been jumped upon causing a 'temporary functional derangement'.

The following two cases illustrate actions which were not held to have amounted to criminal damage:

- in *A (A Juvenile) v R* (1978), a football supporter who spat on a policeman's coat was found not to have committed criminal damage since the coat did not require cleaning or other expenditure;

- a scratch caused to a scaffolding bar did not amount to criminal damage in *Morphitis v Salmon* (1990) since its value or usefulness was not impaired.

Mens rea

The 'basic' s 1(1) offence

The *mens rea* required for the basic offence of criminal damage is an intention to do an act which would cause damage to property belonging to another or being reckless, in the *Caldwell* sense, in relation to such an act.

The 'aggravated' s 1(2) offence

The *mens rea* for this more serious form of criminal damage consists of an intention to damage property and an intention that the damaged property endanger life, or recklessness, in the *Caldwell* sense, as to whether this occurs.

There is no need for life to actually be endangered. All that is required is that the defendant intended the damage to endanger life, or was reckless as to whether this occurred (*R v Dudley* (1989)).

However, the defendant's *mens rea* as to whether life is endangered must extend to the consequences of the criminal damage and not be limited merely to the act causing the damage. For example, in *R v Steer* (1980), the defendant's conviction under s 1(2) for firing rifle shots at the windows of his victim's house was quashed on appeal. There was no evidence that he intended or was reckless as to whether the broken glass, as opposed to the shots themselves, would endanger life.

Defences

Honest belief in the owner's consent is a defence under s 5(2)(a) which provides that a person will have a lawful excuse if:

> ... he believed that the person or persons whom he believed to be entitled to consent to the destruction of or damage to the property in question has so consented, or would have so consented to it if he or they had known of the destruction or damage and its circumstances.

Defence of property

Under s 5(2)(b), the defendant will have a lawful excuse if, in order to protect property, he damaged other property provided he believed that the property was in immediate need of protection and that the means of protection were reasonable in the circumstances.

Section 5(3) clearly provides that the defendant's belief that his actions are reasonable does not itself have to be reasonable. However, the courts have sometimes appeared reluctant to judge defendants on the basis of what they considered to be reasonable in the circumstances (see *Blake v DPP* (1993)).

(5) Offences of deception

- (a) Obtaining property
- (b) Obtaining a money transfer
- (c) Obtaining a pecuniary advantage
- (d) Obtaining services
- (e) Evasion of liability

(a) Obtaining property by deception

Definition

Section 15(1) of the Theft Act 1968 provides:

> A person who by any deception dishonestly obtains property belonging to another, with the intention of permanently depriving the other of it, shall ... be liable ...

Actus reus

Property belonging to another

Section 34(1) provides that s 4(1) and s 5(1) relating to property belonging to another should apply generally for the purposes of the Act. The concepts of 'property' and 'belonging to another', therefore, have a similar meaning to that already noted in relation to s 1 theft.

Obtaining

Section 15(2) provides:

> For the purposes of this section a person is to be treated as obtaining property if he obtains ownership, possession or control of it and 'obtains' includes obtaining for another or enabling another to obtain or to retain.

Clearly, the *actus reus* of the offence will be committed where the defendant induces the victim to sell, give or loan property. However, it seems that the offence would not be committed where the defendant by deception is allowed to retain property of which he already had possession or control. The appropriate charge in these circumstances would be one of theft, by virtue of s 3(1).

However, following the decision in *R v Gomez* (1993), that consent is irrelevant to appropriation, there would now seem to be a large area of overlap between s 1 and s 15.

Section 15(4) provides:

> For the purposes of this section 'deception' means any deception (whether deliberate or reckless) by words or conduct as to fact or as to law, including a deception as to the present intentions of the person using the deception or any other person.

Obviously, to constitute a deception, the statement must be untrue (*R v Deller* (1952)). Moreover, a statement of mere opinion cannot amount to a deception.

A deception can only work on a human mind so a machine cannot be deceived (*Davies v Flackett* (1972)).

Clearly, conduct can amount to a deception (*DPP v Ray* (1974)). A defendant may also deceive by remaining silent where he is aware of a material change in circumstances (*R v Rai* (2000)).

Causation
The deception must be operative in the sense that it must cause the obtaining of the property. It follows that the 'but for' test and other rules relating to causation, noted above, are relevant to deception.

In *R v Collis-Smith* (1971), the defendant, having filled his car with petrol, falsely told a garage attendant that his employer would pay. On appeal, it was held that the deception could not have been operative since it was not made until *after* the property in the petrol had already passed to the defendant. The appropriate charge in these circumstances would have been under s 2 of the 1978 Theft Act (see below).

Mens rea
The *mens rea* for the s 15 offence consists of three elements:

- intention or recklessness (in the *Cunningham* sense) in relation to the deception;

- dishonesty;

- intention to permanently deprive.

Both the *Ghosh* test and the s 6 provisions relating to an intention to permanently deprive apply to the s 15 offence. However, the s 2(1) negative definitions of dishonesty do not apply.

The problem posed by Preddy

In *Preddy* (1996), the House of Lords held that, although the appellants had obtained mortgages by giving false information, the transfer of money between bank accounts did not constitute an offence of obtaining property by deception. Although the effect is exactly the same as if the defendants had obtained property belonging to the victim, since the victim's account is debited and the defendant's account is credited, in law, nothing which formerly belonged to the victim now belongs to the defendant. A chose in action belonging to the victim has been diminished or extinguished and a different chose in action belonging to the defendant has been enlarged or created.

Not only does a money transfer, such as that which took place in *Preddy,* not fall within the ambit of s 15, it also does not constitute theft, since there is no appropriation by the defendant (*R v Caresana* (1996)). Of course, if the defendant has direct control of the victim's bank account and he dishonestly causes transfers to be made from it, there is a theft (*R v Hilton* (1997)).

Since, following *Preddy*, a money transfer brought about by deception will not constitute theft, there is also no stolen property which could be the subject of an offence of handling contrary to s 22 of the Theft Act 1968.

Where a defendant obtains a cheque made out in his favour by deception, there is no offence under s 15, since the chose in action represented by the cheque was never property belonging to another, but, from the moment of its creation, belonged to the defendant. *Preddy* overrules *Duru* (1973) on this point.

(b) Obtaining a money transfer

The Theft (Amendment) Act 1996 plugs the gaps in the law revealed by *Preddy* by inserting s 15A into the Theft Act 1968. This section creates a new offence of obtaining a money transfer by deception which covers the situation where one account is debited and another credited as a result of a deception. This provision would also cover the situation where the defendant obtains a cheque made out to him by deception, since, when the cheque is honoured, there will be a money transfer.

Section 2 of the Theft (Amendment) Act 1996 also adds a new s 24A to the Theft Act 1968. This creates a new offence of dishonestly retaining wrongful credits, which covers instances where transfers of money obtained by deception (now an offence under s 15A of the Theft Act 1968, as amended) are credited to another account. The effect of this provision is that a person who commits an offence under s 15A will also be liable under s 24A if he does not take steps within a reasonable time to divest himself of the wrongful credit. The section will also apply to a defendant who allows 'a wrongful credit' to be transferred to his account.

(c) Obtaining a pecuniary advantage by deception

Definition

Section 16(1) of the Theft Act 1968, as amended, provides:

> A person who by any deception dishonestly obtains for himself or another any pecuniary advantage shall ... be liable ...

Actus reus

The deception must cause the obtaining and 'deception' and 'obtaining' have the same meaning as for s 15 above.

'Pecuniary advantage' does not include any financial benefit, but is limited to the following very specific situations:

- being allowed to borrow by way of overdraft;
- taking out a policy of insurance or annuity contract, or obtaining an improvement of the terms on which the defendant is allowed to do so;
- being given the opportunity to earn remuneration or greater remuneration;
- being given the opportunity to win money by betting.

Mens rea

The requisite *mens rea* consists of two elements:

- intention or recklessness (of the *Cunningham* type) in relation to the deception;
- dishonesty.

The *Ghosh* test as to dishonesty can be given in cases in doubt.

(d) Obtaining services by deception

Definition

Section 1(1) of the Theft Act 1978 provides:

> A person who by any deception dishonestly obtains services from another shall be guilty of an offence.

Actus reus

A 'service' is broadly defined in terms of a 'benefit' that an individual would be willing to pay for (s 1(2)).

'Deception' has the same meaning as in relation to s 15 of the 1968 Theft Act and must be operative in the same way (s 5(1)).

Mens rea

The mental element for this offence consists of an intention or recklessness (in the *Cunningham* sense) in relation to the deception and dishonesty. Once again, in cases of doubt concerning dishonesty, the *Ghosh* direction should be given to the jury.

(e) Evasion of liability by deception

Definitions

Section 2(1) of the Theft Act 1978 creates three offences of evasion of liability by deception. It would appear that the three offences are not mutually exclusive (*R v Holt* (1981)). The offences are committed where a person by deception:

(a) dishonestly secures the remission of the whole or part of any existing liability to make a payment, whether his own liability or another's; or

(b) with intent to make permanent default in whole or in part on any existing liability to make a payment, or with intent to let another do so, dishonestly induces the creditor or any person claiming payment on behalf of the creditor to wait for payment (whether or not the due date for payment is deferred) or to forgo payment; or

(c) dishonestly obtains any exemption from or abatement of liability to make a payment ... shall be guilty of an offence.

Actus reus

As is common to all the deception offences, the deception must be operative in that it must cause the securing of the remission of liability.

The 'liability' must be an existing legal liability to pay with the exception of s 2(1)(c) which encompasses future liabilities (*R v Frith* (1990)).

It would appear that the words 'secured the remission' of the liability in s 2(1)(a) denote nothing less than the total extinguishing of the legal liability to pay. However, it can be argued, as a matter of civil law, that an existing liability can never be extinguished by a deception. This is because any agreement to extinguish liability will be rendered void, or at least, voidable by deception and, therefore, will not be totally extinguished. If this argument is correct, it is difficult to see how anyone could ever be liable in relation to s 2(1)(a).

Notwithstanding the above argument, in *R v Jackson* (1983), the Court of Appeal upheld the defendant's conviction under s 2(1)(a) for using a stolen credit card to pay for petrol and other goods.

Mens rea

The *mens rea* common to all three offences under s 2 is that the defendant should be dishonest and intend to deceive or be reckless, in the *Cunningham* sense, as to whether he deceives. In addition, for the s 2(1)(b) offence, there must also be an intention to make permanent default, in other words, an intention never to pay the debt.

(6) Making off without payment

Definition
Section 3(1) of the Theft Act 1978 provides:

> ... a person who, knowing that payment on the spot for any goods supplied or service done is required or expected from him, dishonestly makes off without having paid as required or expected and with intent to avoid payment of the amount due shall be guilty of an offence.

Actus reus
The offence will not be committed if the payment is not legally enforceable or where the supply of goods or the doing of the service is contrary to law (s 3(3)).

It seems that, for the offence to be complete, the defendant must have 'made off' by leaving the premises where payment is due (*R v McDavitt* (1981)).

Failing to pay includes leaving an inadequate amount, counterfeit notes or foreign currency. It would also include using another's cheque or credit card or leaving a cheque that will be dishonoured. No liability under s 3 arises where the defendant induces the victim to waive the right to payment by exercising a deception (*R v Vincent* (2001)).

Mens rea
The defendant must know that payment on the spot is required and intend to permanently avoid payment and to be dishonest.

(7) Handling stolen goods

Definitions

Section 22 of the Theft Act 1968 provides:

> A person handles stolen goods if (otherwise than in the course of stealing) knowing or believing them to be stolen goods he dishonestly receives the goods, or dishonestly undertakes or assists in their retention, removal, disposal or realisation by or for the benefit of another.

Some of the key terms used in this section are themselves subject to further statutory definition. For example, s 34(2)(b) states that 'goods' include:

> ... money and every other description of property except land and includes things severed from the land by stealing.

From this definition, it would appear that *choses in action*, such as a bank account into which money obtained in exchange for stolen property has been paid, will constitute stolen goods (*R v Pritchley* (1973); *AG's Reference (No 4 of 1979)* (1980)).

In addition, s 24(4) makes it clear that, in order to constitute stolen property, the goods must have been obtained as a result of theft, obtaining property by deception or blackmail.

However, goods will lose their 'stolen' status if they are restored to the person from whom they were stolen or to other lawful possession or custody (s 24(3)). Thus, in *Haughton v Smith* (1975), tins of meat ceased to be 'stolen' when police took control of the lorry transporting them.

What constitutes 'custody' seems to depend on the degree of control exercised over the goods. For example, in *AG's Reference (No 1 of 1974)* (1974), the Court of Appeal were unwilling to hold that a police officer who immobilised a car, that he suspected of containing stolen goods, by removing its rotor arm had taken custody of the property.

In a situation where goods have ceased to be 'stolen' because they have been taken into lawful custody, a defendant who handles them in the belief that they are stolen could be liable for attempting to handle stolen goods contrary to s 1(1) of the Criminal Attempts Act 1981.

It should be noted that, where stolen goods have been exchanged for other forms of property, that other property may also constitute 'stolen goods'. Section 24(2) provides that, for goods to be stolen, they must be, or have been, in the hands of the thief or handler and directly or indirectly represent the stolen goods in whole or in part.

For example, if a stolen picture is exchanged for cash and the cash is then used to buy a car, the picture, the cash and the car are all stolen goods.

B is guilty of handling stolen goods if he knows that the picture was stolen and C is guilty if he knows that the £500 represents the original stolen goods.

Actus reus

Modes of handling

- *Receiving*

   Taking possession of the stolen property. It is not necessary to show that the defendant acted 'for the benefit of another'.

- *Removal*
   Moving the stolen goods from one place to another. The transportation must be for 'the benefit of another'.

- *Realisation*

   Selling or exchanging the stolen goods. The realisation must be 'for the benefit of another'.

- *Disposal*

   Destroying or hiding the stolen goods. The disposal must be 'for the benefit of another'.

- *Retention*

   Keeping possession of the stolen goods. The retention must be 'for the benefit of another'. It seems that a mere omission to inform the police of the presence of stolen property will not amount to retention (*R v Brown* (1970)). However, in *R v Kanwar* (1982), a defendant who deliberately misled the police as to the presence of stolen goods in her home was held to have assisted her husband in their retention.

As well as the above five modes of handling, it is also an offence to arrange to do any of these things or to assist in the removal, realisation, disposal or retention of stolen goods by another person (s 22(1)).

MODES OF HANDLING

Mode	Action	Benefits another	Omission
Receiving	Taking into possession or control	Not necessary	
Removal	Movement of goods	For another's benefit	Action required
Realisation	Sale or exchange of goods		
Disposal	Destroying or hiding		
Retention	Keeping not losing		Possible by omission

NB: Arranging to do any of the above is itself an offence

For the benefit of another

All the above modes of handling, with the exception of receiving and arranging to receive, require that the defendant act 'for the benefit of another'. It follows that a defendant who knowingly sells stolen goods for his own benefit will not be liable for arranging, assisting or undertaking the realisation of stolen property. The innocent purchaser would not be 'another person' within the meaning of the sub-section (*R v Bloxham* (1983)).

Otherwise than in the course of stealing

The above words, included in the definition of the offence, are necessary to prevent many instances of theft from automatically becoming handling as well. Despite the decision of the Court of Appeal in *R v Pitham and Hehl* (1977), it would seem that the phrase 'course of stealing' clearly implies a continuous rather than an instantaneous act. However, such a continuous act concept entails obvious uncertainties about precisely when the act commences and terminates. The practical solution is to allow the jury to decide this matter on a case by case basis.

Mens rea

There are two elements to the *mens rea* of handling: dishonesty and knowledge or belief that the goods are stolen.

In relation to dishonesty, the *Ghosh* test can be applied in cases of difficulty, but should not be automatically resorted to (*R v Roberts* (1987)).

A belief that the property is stolen is a purely subjective matter and should not be equated with what the reasonable person would have believed in the same circumstances (*Atwal v Massey* (1971)).

Where there is evidence that should have made the defendant suspect that the goods were stolen, the jury are entitled to infer a belief that they were stolen (*R v Lincoln* (1980)). However, mere suspicion is not to be equated with such a belief (*R v Grainge* (1974)).

In the absence of a satisfactory explanation to the contrary, a jury is entitled to infer a belief that the property is stolen where there is evidence that the defendant came into possession of the goods soon after the theft.

Dishonestly retaining a wrongful transfer

Section 2 of the Theft Amendment Act 1996 creates a new offence under s 24A of the Theft Act 1968 of 'dishonestly retaining a wrongful transfer. In effect, this creates a new offence of handling.

6 General defences

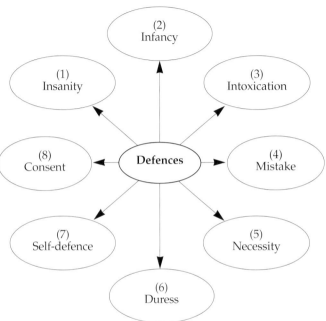

(1) Insanity

Where the defendant claims to have been suffering at the time of the offence from some sort of mental disturbance or impairment, then automatism, insanity and, in murder cases, diminished responsibility may all be considered. Automatism, a condition which consists of the body operating without the control of the mind, and diminished responsibility have been considered above.

Although insanity may also be an issue where the defendant has been remanded in custody, or at the beginning of the trial itself, most undergraduate courses concentrate on insanity in relation to the defendant's mental state at the time of committing the offence. It is insanity as a defence at the trial which is discussed below.

Defence	Nature	When relevant	Effect of successful plea
Automatism	Body acts without control of the mind	At the time of the offence	Not guilty
Diminished responsibility	An abnormality of mind which substantially impairs mental responsibility	At the time of the offence	Not guilty of murder but guilty of manslaughter
Insanity	Disease of the mind which renders the defendant incapable of knowing: (a) the nature and quality of his actions; or (b) that his actions are legally wrong	At the time of the offence	Not guilty Unfit to plead Unfit to plead

It should be noted that insanity, unlike automatism, will not provide a defence to crimes of strict liability (*DPP v H* (1997)).

Definition

In 1843, Daniel M'Naghten, intending to murder Sir Robert Peel, killed his secretary by mistake. Following his acquittal on grounds of insanity, the judges formulated the so called *M'Naghten* rules which have since become accepted as providing a comprehensive definition of insanity (*R v Sullivan* (1984)).

According to these rules, it must be proved (by the defence, on a balance of probabilities) that, at the time the offence was committed, the defendant was labouring under such a defect of reason, arising from a disease of the mind, so as not to know the nature and quality of the act he was doing, or, if he did know it, that he did not know that what he was doing was wrong.

The nature and quality of the act

As we have noted, one of the two grounds for establishing insanity under the *M'Naghten* rules is that the defendant's disease of the mind prevented him from being aware of his actions. For example, in *R v Kemp* (1957), the defendant was found not guilty by reason of insanity when he was unaware of his actions during a 'blackout' caused by a disease of the body which affected the mind.

Did not know that the action was wrong

The second ground for establishing the defence is that, because of a disease of the mind, the defendant did not know that his actions were wrong. 'Wrong', in this context, has been interpreted to mean legally, as opposed to morally, wrong (*R v Windle* (1952)).

Disease of the mind

Although medical evidence will be of relevance, whether a particular condition amounts to a disease of the mind is a legal not a medical question.

It seems that any disease which affects the functioning of the mind is a disease of the mind. Examples would include epilepsy, diabetes, arteriosclerosis and even sleepwalking (*R v Hennessy* (1989); *R v Kemp* (1957); *R v Burgess* (1991)).

In the Canadian case of *Rabey* (1977), it was held that a 'disassociative state' resulting from 'the ordinary stresses and disappointments of life which are the common lot of mankind' did not amount to an external cause. It follows that evidence of such a 'disassociative state' resulting from something qualitatively different to the *ordinary* stresses of life, for example, a rape attack, would indicate an external cause (*R v T* (1990)).

A malfunctioning of the mind is not a disease of the mind if it is caused by some external factor, such as a blow to the head or the consumption of alcohol or drugs (*R v Quick* (1973); *R v Sullivan* (1984)). Such an external cause might form the basis of a plea of non-insane automatism, providing it resulted in a total loss of control of the mind over the body.

(2) Infancy

Rationale

The doctrine of *mens rea* is based on the presumption that criminal liability should only be imposed on those who are capable of understanding the nature and foreseeing the consequences of their actions. Since it is generally assumed that children below a certain age lack this capacity, it follows that they should not be held responsible for acts which if committed by an adult would be criminal.

Children under 10 years of age
There is an *irrebuttable* presumption that a child under the age of 10 at the time of the alleged offence lacks the capacity to form the requisite *mens rea* (s 50 of the Children and Young Persons Act 1933).

Children between the ages of 10 and 14 years of age
There was a presumption, where a child was between the ages of 10 and 14 at the time of the offence, that he or she was not capable of forming the *mens rea* for the crime in question (*C (A Minor) v DPP* (1995)). This presumption could be rebutted if the prosecution could prove not only the *actus reus* and *mens rea*, but also that the child acted with *mischievous discretion*. It would seem that 'mischievous discretion' meant that the child knew that what he or she was doing was seriously wrong (*R v Gorrie* (1919)). This *doli incapax* presumption, as it was known, has now been abolished by s 34 of the Crime and Disorder Act 1998.

Children over 14 years of age
Children over 14 incur criminal liability on proof of *actus reus* and *mens rea* in the same way as adults.

Children and criminal liability

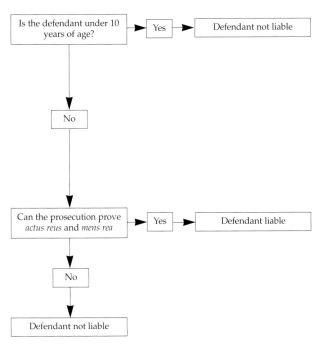

(3) Intoxication

The courts have distinguished between voluntary and involuntary intoxication.

Voluntary intoxication

Self-induced intoxication is not so much a defence, but rather a denial of *mens rea* based upon mistake. Evidence of drunkenness is introduced to make the mistake more credible.

Alcohol and 'dangerous drugs'

Intoxication, negating *mens rea*, resulting from the voluntary consumption of alcohol or drugs generally recognised to be 'dangerous' will constitute a defence to crimes of *specific* intent, but not to those of basic intent (*DPP v Majewski* (1984)).

CRIMES OF SPECIFIC INTENT

Murder
s 18 of the Offences Against the Person Act 1861
s 24 of the Offences Against the Person Act 1861
s 1(2) of the Criminal Damage Act 1971 (where the defendant intends to endanger life)
ss 1, 8, 9, 15, 16, 21, 22, 25 of the Theft Act 1968
ss 2(1)(b), 3 of the Theft Act 1978
s 1 of the Criminal Attempts Act 1981
s 1 of the Criminal Law Act 1977
Incitement

CRIMES OF BASIC INTENT

Assault and battery
ss 20, 23, 47 of the Offences Against the Person Act 1981
Manslaughter
Rape
s 1(1) of the Criminal Damage Act 1971
s 1(2) of the Criminal Damage Act 1971 (where the defendant is reckless as to whether life will be endangered)

Note that s 1(2) of the Criminal Damage Act 1971 is an offence of basic intent if the prosecution allege that it was committed recklessly and one of specific intent if they allege that it was committed intentionally.

It should be noted that, where the defendant deliberately becomes intoxicated with the intention of giving himself 'Dutch courage' in order to commit an offence, the defence will not be allowed (*AG for Northern Ireland v Gallagher* (1963)).

Intoxication other than by alcohol or 'dangerous' drugs

Intoxication, negating *mens rea*, resulting from the voluntary consumption of 'non-dangerous' drugs will constitute a defence not only in relation to crimes of specific intent, but also in relation to those of basic intent, provided the defendant has not been reckless in consuming them (*R v Bailey* (1983); *R v Hardie* (1984)).

The specific/basic intent distinction

Unfortunately, there is no clear overarching principle for distinguishing between crimes of specific and basic intent. However, it is suggested, as a pragmatic guide, that crimes which can be committed recklessly will be those of basic intent and those requiring evidence of intent, specific intent (*MPC v Caldwell* (1982)).

Involuntary intoxication

Involuntary intoxication which negates *mens rea* will be a defence to crimes of both basic and specific intent. Involuntary intoxication which does not negate intent will not provide a defence (*R v Kingston* (1994)).

If the defendant knows that he is drinking alcohol, but is mistaken as to its strength, the rules relating to voluntary intoxication apply (*R v Allen* (1988)).

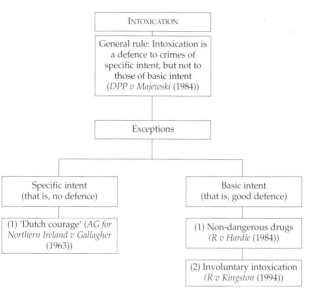

(4) Mistake

Mistake of fact

A mistake of fact is a defence where it prevents the defendant from forming the *mens rea* for the crime in question. For example, if the defendant mistakenly, but honestly, believes that the woman he is having intercourse with consents, he will not be guilty of rape.

The mistake must be an honest one, but it need not be a reasonable one (*DPP v Morgan* (1976)).

Mistake of fact will only avail a defendant if the offence with which he is charged requires proof of *mens rea*. Where a statutory provision creating an offence is silent as to *mens rea* the extent to which mistake of fact will afford a defence depends upon the approach taken by the court to the interpretation of the statute. The House of Lords in *B v DPP* (2000), confirmed that there was a presumption at common law that an offence would not be made out unless *mens rea* was established. The burden will therefore be on the prosecution to establish that the presumption in favour of *mens rea* is displaced either by express words to be found elsewhere in the statute, or by necessary implication – that is, evidence that the statute cannot be as effective as Parliament intended if *mens rea* has to be established. If the presumption in favour of *mens rea* is not displaced the defendant must be judged on the facts as he honestly believed them to be. His belief does not have to be reasonable.

A mistake of fact made while the defendant was intoxicated should be ignored, at least in relation to the defence of self-defence. Thus, in *R v O'Grady* (1987), a defence of self-defence failed where the intoxicated defendant mistakenly believed he needed to defend himself.

(5) Necessity

Rationale

The essence of the defence is that the defendant committed the crime in question in order to avoid an even greater evil. There are two reasons for recognising a defence of necessity in these circumstances:

- it is unjust to punish a defendant for doing something that a reasonable person would have done in the same circumstances; and

- the law should encourage a defendant to choose the lesser and avoid the greater evil on grounds of public policy.

Availability

Despite the above rationale, the courts have traditionally been somewhat reluctant to recognise a full blown defence of necessity. Indeed, in *R v Dudley and Stephens* (1884), Lord Coleridge CJ referred approvingly to Hale's assertion (1 Hale PC 54) that necessity would not be available as a defence to theft of food and then went on to doubt whether it could ever be raised as a defence to homicide.

A distinction can be made between situations where the defendant claims to be acting out of necessity by killing the victim in order to preserve his own life, and the situation where the defendant kills A in order to save the life of B, the defendant not being under any threat of harm himself. In *Re A (Children) (Conjoined Twins: Surgical Separation)* (2000), Brooke LJ stated that in such cases the defence of necessity would be available at common law to a doctor operating to separate conjoined twins, in the knowledge that to do so would cause the death of the weaker twin, provided:

- the defendant's act is needed to avoid inevitable and irreparable evil;
- no more should be done by the defendant than is reasonably necessary for the purpose to be achieved;
- the evil inflicted by the defendant's act must not be disproportionate to the evil avoided.

The statutory defence

The following statutory provisions contain what amounts to the defence of necessity, although it is not often explicitly referred to in this way:

- s 5(2)(b) of the Criminal Damage Act 1971;

- s 1(1) of the Infant Life (Preservation) Act 1929;
- s 1(4) of the Abortion Act 1967.

Necessity at common law

During the 1980s, in cases, such as *R v Willer* (1986); *R v Conway* (1989); and *R v Martin* (1989), the courts have shown a greater willingness to recognise the defence of necessity, initially in relation to road traffic offences, although more recently there has been judicial recognition that the defence is not limited to such cases (*R v Pommell* (1995)).

On the basis of *Conway* and *Martin,* it would appear that, where there is some evidence of necessity, the matter should be left to the jury with the following direction:

- had the defendant felt compelled to act by what he perceived to be the grave danger of the situation? If so,

- would a sober person of reasonable firmness sharing the characteristics of the accused have responded to the perceived threat by acting as the accused had?

If the answers to both these questions are in the affirmative, the defence of necessity, always assuming it to be available, will be established.

(6) Duress

Duress and necessity

The defences of duress and necessity are closely related. Indeed, the courts in cases, such as *Conway* and *Martin* (above), did not explicitly refer to necessity, but to 'duress of circumstances', a phrase also adopted in the Draft Criminal Code Bill of 1989. Although both defences involve a situation where the defendant is faced with a choice of two evils, the major difference between them is the source of the evil. In relation to necessity, the defendant is forced by *circumstances* to break the law, whereas in duress the source of the evil is the threat of another person.

Definition
The defence of duress consists of a plea that the defendant felt compelled to commit a crime because of an immediate threat of death or serious bodily harm by another person. For a successful defence of duress, there has to have been an imminent peril and a direct connection between the threat and the offence charged (*R v Cole* (1994)).

Availability
Because the courts want to encourage people to resist giving in to the pressures to commit crime, they have limited the availability of duress. In particular, the defence is not available in relation to murder or to an accomplice to murder (*R v Howe* (1987)) or in relation to attempted murder (*R v Gotts* (1991)). In addition, the defence is not available in relation to some forms of treason.

The defence of duress will not be available to a defendant if there is evidence that he had the opportunity to get help before the threat was due to be carried out, although regard will be had to his belief as to whether help could have been provided (*R v Hudson and Taylor* (1971)). A threat giving rise to duress can be imminent even though the threat is not one that is going to be carried out there and then (*R v Abdul-Hussain and Others* (1999)).

Also, the defence of duress is not available to those who voluntarily join criminal groups and are then forced to commit the type of crime for which the group is renowned (*R v Sharp* (1987)).

However, if the defendant is forced to commit an offence of a type which he could not have been expected to foresee when he joined the criminal organisation, he may still be able to rely on the defence (*R v Shepherd* (1988)).

Onus of proof

If there are no facts from which the defence might reasonably be inferred in the prosecution's case, then the defendant has to produce some evidence of duress. Once this has been done, the onus of disproving duress rests on the prosecution.

The direction for duress

The direction to be given to the jury where the defendant raises the defence of duress is that laid down by the Court of Appeal in *R v Graham* (1982), as approved by the House of Lords in *R v Howe* (1987).

The jury should consider whether the defendant was compelled to act as he did because, on the basis of the circumstances as he honestly believed them to be, he thought his life was in immediate danger. If so, would a sober person of reasonable firmness sharing the defendant's characteristics have responded in the same way to the threats?

If the answers to both these questions is 'yes', the defence of duress is established. The above direction is very similar to those we have already noted for establishing both necessity and provocation.

A characteristic of the accused of pliability or vulnerability which falls short of psychiatric illness is not a characteristic which can be attributed to the reasonable person for the purposes of the objective limb of the above test (*R v Horne* (1994)).

A mistaken belief of a defendant that he is subject to a threat of death or serious harm can form the basis for the defence of duress. This is so even when the mistaken belief is not a reasonable one (*DPP v Rogers* (1998)).

Coercion

Coercion is a special version of duress which is only available to a wife who commits an offence (other than treason or murder) in the presence of, and under the coercion of, her husband.

The defence appears to be somewhat broader than duress as it encompasses 'pressure' as well as threats of physical violence (*R v Richman* (1982)).

(7) Self-defence and s 3(1) of the Criminal Law Act 1967

The common law allows the citizen to use reasonable force to protect his own person, his property and the person of another. In addition, s 3(1) of the Criminal Law Act 1967 permits the use of reasonable force in order to prevent crime or to arrest offenders.

Self-defence is similar to necessity and duress in the sense that the defendant will be faced with a choice of evils. The defendant will either commit a crime, perhaps homicide or a serious assault, or submit to harm being inflicted on himself, his property or the person of another.

However, unlike necessity and duress, self-defence or s 3(1) can constitute a complete defence to any crime, including murder and treason.

Reasonable force

Only reasonable force may be used in self-defence, defence of property or another, crime prevention and lawful arrest. However, what is reasonable depends upon the circumstances; force which might be reasonable to prevent a violent attack upon the person could be unreasonable in relation to a less serious crime.

In *Re A (Children) (Conjoined Twins: Surgical Separation)* (2000), Robert Walker LJ suggested that if a six year old child firing a gun indiscriminately in a school playground was shot and killed by a defendant to prevent further harm the defendant would be able to rely on the defence of self-defence at common law.

In assessing the reasonableness of the force used, the jury should be directed to take into account the defendant's physical characteristics but not those relating to his mental health (*R v Martin* (2001)).

In *R v Williams (Gladstone)* (1984), it was established that the defendant commits no offence if the force used was reasonable in the circumstances *as he believed them to be*. Thus, it appears that an objective concept of reasonableness was to be applied in the context of a subjective interpretation of the circumstances (*R v Owino* (1995)).

(8) Consent

Scope

Although most textbooks consider consent in relation to assaults, it should be remembered that the consent of the owner is a complete defence to theft – although, since *Gomez*, consent does not negate the *actus reus* of theft, an honest belief in the consent of the owner will negate *mens rea* (s 1(2)(b)) and criminal damage. Moreover, sexual offences, such as rape, usually require proof not only that the victim was not consenting, but also that the accused knew or was reckless as to this lack of consent.

Availability
On grounds of public policy, the courts have restricted the availability of the defence. Consent is not available in relation to:

- murder or manslaughter (even if the victim begs to be killed because he is terminally ill and in intense pain);

- a fight, other than in the course of an organised sport, played according to the rules (*AG's Reference (No 6 of 1980)* (1981));

- the deliberate infliction of bodily harm for no good purpose (*R v Brown and Others* (1993)).

However, the courts are prepared to allow the defence in relation to:

- lawful sporting activities according to the rules;

- medical and dental treatment carried out by qualified practitioners;

- rough horseplay, where the victim has consented to the risk of harm (*R v Jones* (1987); *R v Atkin and Others* (1992));

- tattooing and, it would appear, the type of branding which occurred in *R v Wilson* (1996), where a man branded his initials on his wife's buttocks at her request.

Consent and mistake
An honest belief (but not necessarily a reasonable belief) that the victim was consenting will negate the *mens rea* of the

defendant (*DPP v Morgan* (1976); *R v Kimber* (1983)). Of course, this is provided the offence in question is one where the defence of consent is recognised.

Consent obtained by deception
If the consent of the victim was obtained by deception or fraud, it will be a valid defence provided it relates to a *non-fundamental* matter, but will be void where it relates to a *fundamental* matter (*R v Williams* (1923)).

A fundamental mistake occurs where the victim consents to something which is *qualitatively* different to that which he thought he was consenting to. For example, if A consents to have sexual intercourse with B in the mistaken belief that B is a film star, the consent will still be valid. A is not fundamentally mistaken about the nature of the act, there is merely a non-fundamental mistake about the status of B. However, if A believes that what they are going to do is a yoga exercise, then she is fundamentally mistaken about the nature of the activity and her consent will be rendered void (*R v Richardson* (1999)).

A woman who mistakenly believes that she is consenting to sexual intercourse with her husband or boyfriend will have made a fundamental mistake (*R v Elbekkay* (1995)).